THE CHALLENGE of the CULTS

A *Christianity Today* Symposium

by

Harold Lindsell
Wesley P. Walters
Walter R. Martin
Peter Fingesten
John H. Gerstner
J. K. Van Baalen
Wilbur M. Smith
Lit-Sen Chang

ZONDERVAN PUBLISHING HOUSE
Grand Rapids, Michigan

Second printing — September, 1961

Most of the articles herein contained first appeared in the Dec. 19, 1960 issue of *Christianity Today*. The article on Spiritualism, however, is from the Jan. 16, 1961 issue, and the one on Zen-Buddhism, while prepared and edited for the magazine, appears here for the first time in printed form.

Printed in the United States of America

CONTENTS

Are the Cults Outpacing Our Churches?

HAROLD LINDSELL

Wherever one moves in American religious circles, one hears the refrain that the lively cults are making tremendous progress at the expense of listless Protestant churches. Hence, the impression has arisen that the cults have greater vitality, are outstripping the regular denominations, and are winning more converts from among the unchurched. There is real need, therefore, to examine the growth of the cults to see whether these generally accepted conclusions are valid.

If one were to rate the cults on the basis of numerical growth over the past decade, one would be entirely incorrect to call them "lively" and the regular churches "listless." A summary of statistics for the past 10 years will prove enlightening.

STATISTICS OF GROWTH

Numerically the largest of all the cults is Mormonism which embraces several groups of people under its general label. In 1950 the aggregate church membership figure for all of these segments was 1,184,000. In 1960 the aggregate was 1,550,000 (all figures have been taken from *World Almanac*). This meant a net increase of 366,000. Percentage-wise the growth during the decade was a little over 30 per cent.

Harold Lindsell is Dean of the Faculty and Professor of Missions at Fuller Theological Seminary. He holds the B.S. from Wheaton College, M.A. from University of California, and Ph.D. from New York University. Latest of his books is *Daily Bible Readings from the Revised Standard Version.*

Another cult is Seventh-day Adventism (some will dispute whether this group is truly a cult). In 1950 its membership was given as 225,000. In 1960 it was 305,000. The rate of growth was 36 per cent.

The Church of Christ, Scientist, is probably the second or third largest cult in the United States. It probably has a larger membership than Seventh-day Adventism, although this is not certain. Christian Science membership statistics are not generally made public. However, during World War II the church was required to reveal its membership figures to the Government in order to obtain the proper number of appointments to the chaplaincy of the armed forces. At that time the membership figure was given as 268,900. Assuming a growth rate of 50 per cent for the decade and a half since the figure was released, we may approximate 403,000 for the membership of the cult today.

The next largest cult is Jehovah's Witnesses for which no 1950 membership figures are available in the United States. However, in 1951 the world-wide figure stood at about 440,000. In 1960 the Jehovah's Witnesses main office supplied accurate figures for its membership in the United States: the total was 239,000. While it is impossible to estimate the percentage increase, one may reasonably suppose that the movement did not gain more than 50 per cent during the decade.

The Spiritualists claimed 126,000 members in 1950 and 175,000 in 1960. The rate of growth was 40 per cent. Unitarians claimed 75,000 for 1950 and 108,000 for 1960. The rate of growth was about 44 per cent. The Universalists numbered 44,600 in 1950 and 69,000 in 1960. The rate of growth was 54 per cent. The Swedenborgians lost ground with 7,000 members in 1950 but only 6,000 in 1960. Buddhists reported 70,000 in 1950 and only 10,000 in 1960. (These statistics must be regarded with suspicion, for the marked reversal suggests possible inaccuracy.) The Baha'is had fewer than 4,500 members in 1950. They provided no statistics for 1960. The Rosicrucians provided no figures for 1950 but listed 45,000 for 1960. The Christadelphians listed 2,755 for 1950 and 15,000 for 1960. The round figures for the latter year are open to question. No statistics are available for either the Unity School of Christianity or Theosophy for 1950 and 1960.

SOME OBSERVATIONS

On the basis of the membership figures for the cults, one may make two generalizations. First, in 1950 the cults included in their membership no more than 2,500,000. Secondly, in 1960 a generous estimate of the total membership of all the cults put together would be 3,200,000, which is about three per cent of the number acknowledging church or cult connections.

Up to this point the statistics, by themselves, neither prove nor disprove the concept of "lively" cults and "listless" churches. If, for example, Protestant church membership declined 50 per cent during the same decade in which the cults increased 30 or 35 per cent, such a description would be very apt. If Protestant church membership remained static, the implication would still be approximately correct. But if the membership of Protestant churches advanced during the same period the cults did, then the assumption would be incorrect. Thus our attention must be focused on the growth of the cults in relation to the growth or decline of the Protestant churches.

Let us consider the two largest Protestant church groups in America: the Methodists and the Southern Baptists. The Methodist Church had a membership of approximately 8,900,000 in the 1950 *World Almanac* report. The membership increased to 9,800,000 in 1960. The rate of growth was slightly better than 10 per cent. The Southern Baptist Convention reported a membership of approximately 6,500,000 in 1950. By 1960 it had increased to 9,200,000. The rate of growth was 41 per cent. In the membership of the American Baptist Convention, there was a slight decline which may be accounted for by the fact that the Convention was in the process of schism in view of the departure from the American Baptist Convention of the Conservative Baptist Association which reported a membership of 275,000 in 1960.

The various Presbyterian bodies claimed 3,500,000 members in 1950 and an increase to 4,140,000 in 1960. The rate of growth was slightly less than 20 per cent. The membership of the Reformed bodies increased from 319,000 to 459,000; their growth rate was more than 40 per cent. The Pentecostal Assemblies reported a membership of 169,000 in 1950, and added some 223,000 in the 10 year span to reach an aggregate of 392,000 members in the 1960 report. The rate of growth was 132 per cent.

THE ADVANCE OF ROMANISM

During the same 1950-1960 decade, the Roman Catholic church grew appreciably. It claimed a baptized membership of 26,700,000 in 1950, and in 1960 the church placed it at around 39,500,000. The growth factor was close to 50 per cent.

The combined statistics for all religious bodies indicate that membership increased from about 82,500,000 in 1950 to 109,000,000 in 1960. This means that the growth rate was 33 1/3 per cent. With such a background it is possible to draw certain tentative conclusions. First, the Roman Catholic church enjoyed a better than average rate of growth in the past decade. Secondly, if its rate of growth continues without equal Protestant growth, the Roman church will eventually become the dominant religious force in American life. Our third conclusion is that the cults have not, in fact, been "lively" so far as actual numerical growth is concerned. They have averaged about the same percentage as the national figure for the Protestant churches. Our fourth conclusion is that the "listless" churches have not been as "listless" as supposed but have enjoyed a substantial growth in the last 10 years.

The Southern Baptist membership alone increased by some 2,700,000. The membership of the Methodist Church increased by about 900,000. Furthermore, the smaller Protestant denominations enjoyed good growth.

The Baptist General Conference, the Christian and Missionary Alliance, the Evangelical Mission Covenant Church, the Evangelical Free Churches, The General Association of Regular Baptist Churches, and the Mennonite bodies increased from approximately 400,000 to approximately 500,000.

The growth of the cults has not been disproportionate to the growth of Protestant groups in general. One must acknowledge, of course, that the larger the group the less apt it is to have a large percentage growth, even though its numerical increase may be much larger than smaller groups with higher percentage increases. For example, additions to the churches of the Southern Baptist Convention alone were about four times the aggregate number of new adherents to the cults. Since it cannot be demonstrated that the cults are "lively" and the churches "listless" according to numerical gains, in what sense are we able to say that the adjectives are true?

VITALITY OF THE CULTS

One cannot help being impressed by the publishing activities of many of the cults. Jehovah's Witnesses publish the magazines *Watchtower* and *Awake* and industriously disseminate them. Millions of copies of books written by men like Charles Taze Russell have come from their presses. There is probably no other religious group of its size in America that uses the printing press more extensively than the Jehovah's Witnesses. The Unity School of Christianity and Seventh-day Adventism also take advantage of the printed page to press their claims before the American public. One of the easiest ways to get an idea of the vast amount of literature being made available by the cultists is to check the card index of an average public library. One will see how much has been done via the medium of expression.

A second way in which the "lively" cults surpass the "listless" churches is in personal missionary work. Numerous instances may be mentioned. Every Mormon gives two years of his life for direct missionary work during which time he forsakes his normal occupation in order to spread the tenets of his cult. Jehovah's Witnesses claim that every member of the cult is a "minister." In my own experience, I have observed that the representatives of the Jehovah's Witnesses showed more zeal in my area than any or all of the Protestant denominations in the past 13 years. No Baptist, Methodist, Presbyterian, Lutheran, Episcopalian, or other Protestant ever rang my doorbell; but advocates from Jehovah's Witnesses came at least a dozen times to sell printed material, press their claims, or in other ways represent the cult. Christian Scientists in almost every community maintain book rooms where one may sit down in quiet to read the interpretation of the Word of God according to Mary Baker Eddy. How many Protestant churches maintain book rooms in their sanctuaries or in the stores along the main streets to reach men with the gospel of Christ?

Thirdly, the "lively" cults are outdoing the Protestants in the field of communications, such as radio and television. Adventists, Mormons, Jehovah's Witnesses, and others maintain expensive broadcasts which reach into the homes of millions of people. Free literature is advertised for the asking. Adventists offer a free Bible correspondence course which enrolls thousands of people unperceptive of the differences between Adventism and evangelical Protestantism. The Christadelphians maintain a radio broadcast as does the Rutherford, New Jersey, splinter group from the Jehovah's Witnesses "Frank and Ernest" program.

When such activities are compared with the communication activities of the Protestant denominations, it soon becomes apparent that the cults, for their size, are manifesting an aggressive zeal and enjoying an outreach far beyond anything being done by the denominations.

It is at these points that the cults are "lively" and the churches "listless." For sheer enthusiasm, dynamic outreach, and zealous abandonment, the cultist puts the average Protestant to shame. Yet the cults do not seem to have gathered a return in proportion to their multiplied activities. Evidence would suggest that if the denominations would embark on programs as extensive for their sizes as those of the cults in relation to their sizes, they would produce a far larger harvest than has been the case in the last decade. Therefore, if the denominations do not step up their efforts in reaching people for the gospel of Christ, we may find in another generation a staggering new growth of the cults which are now sowing seeds for harvest.

Christian Science

JOHN H. GERSTNER

The essential history of Christian Science may be reduced to three epochal phases: first, Mary Baker Eddy's discovery of the principles of Christian Science; second, her establishment of the religion which bears that name; and, third, the cult's organizational solidification following her death. It seems that after a long period of personal and domestic vicissitudes, as well as ill health, Mrs. Eddy came to believe in spiritual healing through Phineas B. Quimby in 1862. Many non-Scientists argue that she got her basic healing system from him and others, but her followers maintain that ultimately she discovered a radically different system which came by divine revelation and was recorded in her definitive volume, *Science and Health with Key to the Scriptures,* first published in 1875. As a result, the Christian Science Church was founded, followed by the establishment of the Massachusetts Metaphysical College in 1881. Societies and churches were built, publishing houses were established, and the religion spread around the world. Mrs. Eddy died in 1910 at 89 years of age. Thousands revered her, others respected her, still others condemned her, and all acknowledged that she was one of the outstanding women of religious history. The story of Christian Science after the time of Mrs. Eddy has been told fully, at least in

John H. Gerstner is Professor of Church History in Pittsburgh Theological Seminary. He holds the B.A. from Westminster College, B.D. and B.Th. from Westminster Theological Seminary, and Ph.D. from Harvard University. He is author of six books, including *The Theology of the Major Sects.*

certain aspects, by Altman K. Swihart in *Since Mrs. Eddy* (1931) and by Charles Braden in *Christian Science Today* (1958). The books show that the Board of Directors have consolidated the organization which the foundress began into one of the most efficient authoritarian and rigid structures known to religious history.

Christian Science has enjoyed a steady but not uninterrupted growth since the time of its inception. Dr. Braden, who has computed his statistics from the *Christian Science Journal,* calculates that "the Church of Christ, Scientist, with its total of 3,115 churches and societies, would have a world membership of 367,570." Below is his table of churches throughout the world.

YEAR	Africa	Asia	Australia	Europe	Great Britain	Canada	United States
1911	5	2	7	15	68	35	1,190
1919	7	3	9	22	94	46	1,684
1922	3	3	10	35	120	47	1,635
1931	22	7	35	94	219	66	2,030
1941	35	13	48	150	313	74	2,284
1958	40	13	70	175*	344	79	2,372

**The total does not include churches in East Germany.*

Christian Science, along with the Jehovah's Witnesses, Church of the Latter Day Saints, and other sects, joins with the traditional churches in affirming the inspiration of the Bible (*Science and Health,* pp. 126 f., 269 f., and so on). But like the sectarian groups and unlike the evangelical churches, it affirms other inspired sources alongside the Bible which indeed supplant the Bible. If Mrs. Eddy's *Science and Health with Key to the Scriptures* is a true key to the Bible, then the historic churches have been in error for 20 centuries. Christian Scientist Arthur J. Todd, in saying that there are four religious groups in the United

States, namely, Roman Catholic, Protestant, Jewish, and Christian Scientist, rightly sensed that the religion taught by Mrs. Eddy is something other than what the historic churches have understood to be taught by the Bible. The reason for the difference is that Christian Science does not believe in the inspiration of the Bible *only* but of Mrs. Eddy *also* (*Science and Health*, pp. 560 f.).

DOCTRINAL DEVIATIONS

Let us note then the crucial doctrine of Christian Science, namely the doctrine of God. "God is incorporeal, divine, supreme, infinite Mind, Spirit, Soul, Principle . . ." (*Science and Health*, pp. 465 f. passim). Mrs. Eddy deduces from the biblical principle of the infinity of God that he is not personal. "Limitless personality is inconceivable" (*No and Yes*, p. 20; *Science and Health*, pp. 265, 331). According to George Channing, an authoritative spokesman for the religion, God is not Triune but "Life, Truth, and Love are 'the triune Principle called God'" ("What is a Christian Scientist?," *Look*, Nov. 18, 1952, p. 57). The Father tends to be identified with God more than anything or anyone else is, although a common tenet of Christian Science is that All is God and God is All. As for the Second Person in the Trinity, the Son of God, Mary Baker Eddy writes: "The Christian believes that Christ is God . . . Jesus Christ is not God" (*Science and Health*, p. 361). By this she means that Christ is the Principle and as such is identified with God; Jesus is the corporeal man with great insight into the Principle but as corporeal man not identified with God. As for the Third Person of the Trinity, the Holy Spirit is Christian Science. "This Comforter I understand to be Divine Science" (*Science and Health*, p. 55).

Since God is All, and man, the true or spiritual man, is part of God, man possesses the attributes of God. "He is co-existent with God. As far back as the being of God is the being of man. 'Searching for the origin of man is like enquiring into the origin of God himself, the self-existent and eternal'" (Haldeman, *Christian Science,* p. 112; *Science and Health,* p. 535). "Hence," writes Gilmore, another Scientist authority, "the real man as God's likeness, without material accompaniments, has existed forever. When Jesus asserted, 'Before Abraham was, I am,' he undoubtedly referred to his true selfhood as the Son of God, as the Christ-man" (Braden, *Varieties of American Religion,* p. 163).

Christian Science denies the death of Jesus Christ. *Science and Health* renders Romans 5:8 as, ". . . we were reconciled to God by the (seeming) death of His Son" (p. 45). Since Christ did not provide a perfect atonement, it is not surprising that we read: "The atonement requires constant self-immolation on the sinner's part" (pp. 23, 24).

The most important application of the Christian Scientist doctrine of salvation is, of course, to healing. "Man is never sick, for Mind is not sick and matter cannot be" (*Science and Health,* p. 393). "Sin and disease," writes Gilmore, "are figments of the mortal or carnal mind, to be destroyed, healed, by knowing their unreality." Thus Christian Science is not a system of religious healing through medicine (which presupposes real sickness) nor a system of faith healing (because it does not believe in healing actual sickness by some special power from God) but of Mind Cure or the proving to the Mind, and thereby producing in the experience, that the sickness is unreal.

The need for healing and salvation continues into

the next world. "If the change called *death* destroyed the belief in sin, sickness, and death, happiness would be won at the moment of dissolution, and be forever permanent; but this is not so. . . . The sin and error which possess us at the instant of death do not cease at that moment, but endure until the death of these errors. . . . Universal salvation rests on progression and probation, and is unattainable without them. Heaven is not a locality but a divine state of Mind in which all the manifestations of Mind are harmonious and immortal. . . . No final judgment awaits mortals, for the judgment-day of wisdom comes hourly and continually . . ." (*Science and Health*, pp. 290 f.).

CRITIQUE OF TEACHING

1. The fundamental fallacy of Christian Science teaching which vitiates its entire theology is the doctrine of God. As indicated above, its basic proposition is that God is All, which is all wrong. The first verse of the Bible refutes it. In the beginning God created the heavens and the earth. There is a temporal allusion here in the words "in the beginning," for the reference is to the beginning of the heaven and the earth. But God has no beginning any more than he has an end. The universe, therefore, being temporal is other than God who is eternal. God is said to have created or made the world. But God himself is not made or created. The universe, therefore, being created is other than God who is uncreated. *Barah* (create) indicates a making out of nothing or *ex nihilo*. God is pure Being. The universe, therefore, being created from nothing is other than God who is eternal Being. The biblical doctrine of God does not teach that he is All, but that he is *in* all. This is a vastly different teaching for if God is in all he cannot be all. "In" all does not identify him with the all, but, on the contrary, distinguishes him from it.

2. *"Mortal Mind" is the bastard offspring of the illegitimate union of God with All.* And like all bastards Mortal Mind is a source of perpetual embarrassment to its parents. Mortal Mind is used by Christian Science to explain away all evil; that is, all evil, which is supposedly nonexistent, is said to be the illusory product of the Mortal Mind. But Mortal Mind itself is never explained away. It is, therefore, the ultimate source of "evil" in this world. It is itself the most evil thing in the world. The Scientists dare not explain it away because it is necessary for explaining all other evil away. So this ultimate evil must be real in order to explain the unreality of all other evil. If it is said to be unreal then all other evil comes alive again. Mortal Mind is the nemesis of the cult's theology: Christian Science cannot explain it or explain it away; it cannot affirm it or deny it; it cannot live with it or without it. Mortal Mind is mortal to Christian Science—the Frankenstein which destroys its creator.

3. *Christian Science has taken away our Saviour and we know not where it has laid him.* His body is not real, being physical: his death is not real, being physical and evil; his humanity is not real, being limited and capable of ignorance; even his divinity is not real (in the true sense of the word) for all men are essentially divine and God is essentially human because God is All and All is God and man and everything. To preserve the terms of orthodox theology so as to deceive, if it were possible, the very elect, is a vain effort to cover the nakedness of this Christology with the fig leaves of empty verbiage.

4. *Lastly, we mention the weakness of the Christian Science theory of Mind cure.* On the surface the system

must be fallacious since it derives from a theology which is fallacious. Is it possible to get good fruit from a bad tree, sound therapy from unsound theology? Manifestly not. Still, let the reader not jump to the wrong conclusion that we have now denied any and all Christian Science healings. We deny that any true healing could come from a fallacious premise such as Christian Science. But this is not the same as saying that no healing may come by Christian Scientists. From their own viewpoint, sickness (a form of evil) is erroneous, that is, nonexistent. Christian Scientists may thereby bring about some cures, not because Christian Science is true but because its formula happens to fit particular patients. Many patients have nothing wrong with them. Their pains are imaginary, their ailments subjective. If you convince such patients of this by sugar pills, suggestion, Spiritualism, Christian Science, or whatever, you will likely cure them. But there is as much connection between your Christian Science and his cure as there is between the famous rooster's crowing and the rising of the sun. The sun rose when the rooster crowed, to be sure, but the event gave the *rooster* nothing to crow about.

SELECTION OF BOOKS FOR STUDY

The main sources for information about Christian Science are of course the writings of Mary Baker Eddy: *Miscellaneous Writings* (1896), *The Science of Man* (1870), *Essays on Christian Science, Church Manual* (1895-1910), and especially, *Science and Health with Key to the Scriptures* (1875). The *Christian Science Sentinel* and *Christian Science Journal* are authorized periodicals. The authorities stamp certain volumes "authorized," which is the Christian Science *Imprimatur*. The authorized lives of Mrs. Eddy are by Sibyl Wilbur and Lyman P. Powell.

Many other books make for profitable reading:

Edwin Franden Dakin, *Mrs. Eddy, The Biography of a Virginal Mind* (1930) – a penetrating critique.

H. A. L. Fisher, *Our New Religion* (1930) – the work of an able and slightly amused Englishman.

Georgine Milmine, *The Life of Mary Baker G. Eddy and the History of Christian Science* (1909) – difficult to find, but invaluable.

James H. Snowden, *The Truth about Christian Science* (1920) – the best full-length historico-theologico-philosophical examination.

Walter R. Martin and Norman H. Klann, *The Christian Science Myth* – the latest evangelical study.

Wilbur Smith, "The Bible in Christian Science Literature" (*Sunday School Times,* Feb. 9, 1952) – should be consulted along with the chapters in general works on The Sects.

Mormonism

WESLEY P. WALTERS

Almost anywhere in America today one may see two alert, conservatively-dressed young men, knocking on doors and approaching their prospect pleasantly with, "We are from the Church of Jesus Christ of Latter-day Saints." By means of the best modern sales techniques, these somewhat mysterious and intriguing figures of the "Mormon" Church then offer a religion that claims to be the only authentic church of God, restored in these latter days by God and Christ in person, by angels, and by Peter, James, and John. They boast an extraordinarily well-organized welfare system and a love of culture and the good things of life. Using the standard Christian terms, they speak of the Godhead, of gospel and glory, of sin and salvation, of prophets and patriarchs—but they put into them a meaning radically different from that found in the Bible.

HISTORICAL DEVELOPMENT

The group's verifiable history begins in upper New York state in the year 1830 with the publication of the *Book of Mormon* by Joseph Smith, Jr., an able young man with little formal education. The publication of the book is represented to be the culmination of several "visions" and "revelations." Smith's first "vision" (allegedly received in 1820 but not published until 20

Wesley P. Walters is Minister of Marissa United Presbyterian Church in Illinois. He holds the B.S. degree from Johns Hopkins University and the B.D. from Reformed Episcopal Seminary. A student of the cults, he flew to Salt Lake City for a week to substantiate his facts with Mormon leaders.

years later and now somewhat altered) informed him that all churches are wrong and all their creeds an abomination. The subsequent "revelations" led to the "discovery" and "translation"—by means of the "Urim and Thummim"—of "gold plates" which were buried in a near-by hill and contained the *Book of Mormon.* Echoing an idea current in Smith's day that the Indians were descendants of the lost tribes of Israel, the book basically relates how they came to America (about 600 B.C.), were visited by the Saviour, and fell into their present primitive state.

Like the word "Mormon" itself, which Smith derived from the English "more" and the (supposed) Egyptian "mon" meaning "good" (*Times and Seasons,* Vol. IV, p. 194), the book was an odd blending of the contemporary scene and the fictitious past, generously sprinkled with passages lifted bodily from the King James Version. A year after its publication, Alexander Campbell observed that in the book, supposedly completed by 421 A.D., Smith had written "every error and almost every truth discussed in New York for the last 10 years. He decides all the great controversies—infant baptism, ordination, the Trinity . . . and even the question of freemasonry, republican government, and the rights of man." Because the book borrows so heavily from the theology of the day, it is considerably more orthodox than Smith's later productions, causing noticeable internal conflict in Mormon doctrine.

With the work completed and the translation declared "correct" by the "Lord," the plates allegedly were returned to heaven safe from prying eyes after being "viewed" by a few chosen witnesses. (Some 3200 improvements have since been made, mostly grammatical, but about 100 change the meaning.) By

1830 Joseph Smith had begun his new church which was named, in good *Book of Mormon* and Campbellite fashion, "The Church of Christ." Writing again in 1838, Smith claimed that in 1829 John the Baptist had appeared and restored to him the "Aaronic Priesthood" and a few weeks later Peter, James, and John restored the "Melchizedek Priesthood." The Melchizedek Priesthood forms the chief source of authority for the church's hierarchy and for nearly all the temple ceremonies. However, references to its high priests, high counselors, and presidents are conspicuously absent from Smith's "revelations" on church government as first printed in 1833 in the *Book of Commandments.* Like many other matters, references to this priesthood first appear interpolated back into the early revelations when reprinted in the 1835 *Doctrine and Covenants* (cf. LaMar Petersen, *Problems in Mormon Texts,* 1957). Overlooking the biblical application of the Melchizedek Priesthood to Christ *alone* (fulfilling and superseding the earthly Aaronic priesthood), Smith claims to have received more of its authority from visits in 1836 by both Elijah and Elias (two separate persons to Smith! — cf. *Doctrine and Covenants,* 27.6, 9).

The *Book of Mormon* indicates that "plain and precious parts" of the Bible have been taken away by a corrupt church. Smith set about the task of restoring these parts by "revelation and inspiration." The result was an "inspired" revision of the Bible, completed in 1833 but not published until 1867. The early chapters of Genesis received considerable reworking and are published separately as *The Book of Moses.* About 1835, however, Smith began to study Hebrew, and, learning that Elohim (God) was plural, he soon brought forth a new version of the Genesis creation story. This version was his "translation" of a papyrus written by "Abraham" himself and acquired, along with an Egyptian mummy, from a traveling showman. In it the "gods" create the heavens and the earth. The *Book of Abraham* together with the *Book of Moses* and excerpts from Smith's autobiography form the volume known as *The Pearl of Great Price.* That volume along with the *Bible, Book of Mormon,* and *Doctrine and Covenants* form the "Standard Works" of the Mormon Church in Utah.

Like leaders of other groups in the early nineteenth century, Smith believed that Christ's coming was imminent, "even 56 years should wind up the scene" (*Millenial Star,* Vol. 15, p. 205). It was necessary for the "saints," he revealed, to gather to Zion to escape the destruction coming upon the wicked, and the revelation disclosed that Independence, Missouri, was that place. However, they were driven from there by aroused "gentiles" in 1833. Then Far West, Missouri, was the chosen spot, a place not far from Adam-ondi-Ahman where, Smith revealed, the original Garden of Eden once stood and Adam's altar was still to be seen. Ordered out of Missouri, however, in 1838, the saints followed the call to gather in Nauvoo, Illinois (George B. Arbaugh, *Gods, Sex and Saints,* p. 12 f.; cf. *Doctrine and Covenants,* 57.1-3, 115.5-7, 125.2), only to be driven from there after Smith was killed in 1844 by an angry mob. Finally, under Brigham Young, some of the saints discovered that the Salt Lake Valley was "the place."

CURRENT DIVISIONS

In Utah the church has thrived, acquiring commercial holdings running into millions of dollars, operating a 60-million-dollar, up-to-date university (Brigham Young), and sponsoring a large-scale welfare program for its own people. Its world membership is now placed at about 1,650,000. Since the days when Smith offered "eternal salvation" to individuals whom he called by revelation to be missionaries, the church has maintained a strong proselytizing program. With better than 7500 "missionaries" on the field—mostly college-age youths donating two years of service—the church expects in the reasonable future to reach a goal of 12,000 missionaries and to see advances particularly in India and the surrounding countries.

Of the more than dozen groups which rose after Smith's death to claim divine authority as his successor, the Reorganized Church of Jesus Christ of Latter Day Saints is the second largest that survives. Numbering about 200,000, with headquarters in Independence, Missouri, the Reorganized Church does not accept the *Book of Abraham* with its plurality of gods, or the revelation sanctioning polygamy; and therefore it is somewhat closer to historic Christianity. Another group, the Church of Christ (also in Independence), uses the *Book of Commandments* instead of the *Doctrine and Covenants* and holds (along with David Whitmer, one of the *Book of Mormon* witnesses) that after 1833 Joseph Smith became a "fallen prophet" and changed the structure and theology of the church.

THEOLOGICAL DEVELOPMENTS

One area where the theological shift becomes very evident is in the Mormon doctrine of deity. In the *Book of Mormon* and earlier revelations, God is often displayed with such unity that the Son *is* the Father. In later productions the Father and Son emerge as two separate "flesh and bone" beings, united in sharing common qualities and purposes. Finally, men themselves are declared to be able by means of temple ceremonies to progress to Godhood. Out of eternal matter they will shape other worlds and people them, just as the Father peopled this one, by "spirit children" born to their wives. In the early days in Utah this type of teaching reached such an extreme that Adam was held to be the God of this world and Jesus was not born of the Holy Spirit but by the physical union of this Adam-God with Mary (*Journal of Discourses*, Vol. I, p. 50). These one-time gems of heavenly light are looked upon by many modern Mormons as the unwise "speculations" of the early leaders. The "Godhead" today is represented as consisting of two separate personages with flesh and bone bodies and the Holy Ghost with a "body of spirit." The Son has the distinction of being the first of many "spirit children" born to the heavenly Father and "Mother." Like the Father, who is an exalted and "perfected man" living near the planet "Kolob," each spirit child must come to earth and take a "physical body" in order to progress toward Godhood: his pre-existent faithfulness determines what race and status he should be born into here.

Tied inseparably to the Mormon concept of deity is the Mormon idea of salvation. For the most part the biblical doctrine of sin is replaced with the idea of sins (for example, smoking, drinking alcohol, coffee, tea), none of which merit everlasting punishment. Salvation, therefore, becomes a matter of striving to reach the highest degree of glory, that is, Godhood itself. The path upward begins with repentance (mainly of the above sins), Mormon baptism, laying on of hands, and church membership. However, the highest or celestial glory can only be reached through the various temple ceremonies. In the temple, living Mormons may go through baptism and the other ceremonies on behalf of their dead relatives and thus deliver their spirits from the "prison house" and enable them to progress toward exaltation. But the pinnacle of celestial glory, Godhood itself, can only be reached through the temple ceremony that claims (contrary to Christ's express teaching in Luke 20.34 f.) to seal husbands and wives in marriage for time *and eternity*. This doctrine is based on the teaching in Smith's revelation sanctioning polygamy, in which he made Godhood dependent on man's ability to beget innumerable children throughout eternity (*Doctrine and Covenants*, 132.15-19, 63). Since obviously this can best be accomplished by having a plurality of wives, Smith received the "divine" command to seal many wives to himself and his followers. Today the church advises its members in America to refrain from contracting polygamous marriages because it is forbidden by the government, but the principle of polygamy remains on their books as divinely approved.

The teaching that the sex relationship continues in the eternal state has yielded a strong practical emphasis on home and family solidarity, but it has robbed the religion of any real spiritual relationship with the Lord. In seeking exaltation through physical relationships and ceremonious activities, Mormonism completely misses real salvation *and exaltation* as a free gift of God's grace. The Gospel is reduced to laws and ordinances brought to men by a Christ whose only function as Saviour is to guarantee to men a resurrection. To those enmeshed in a religion so materialistic in emphasis and so lacking in reverence, evangelical Christianity must hold out an all-sufficient Saviour who saves, sanctifies, *and glorifies* unworthy sinners who place all their confidence in Him alone.

SELECTION OF BOOKS FOR STUDY

Mormon

Gordon B. Hinckely, *What of the Mormons* (Church of Jesus Christ of L.D.S., 1954).

Bruce R. McConkie, *Mormon Doctrine* (Bookcraft, 1958).

James E. Talmage, *The Articles of Faith* (Church of Jesus Christ of L.D.S., 1958).

Non-Mormon

George B. Arbaugh, *Gods, Sex and Saints* (Augustana, 1957).

Fawn M. Brodie, *No Man Knows My History* (Knopf, 1946) – Smith's biography, documented, by L.D.S. President's niece.

Gordon H. Fraser, *Is Mormonism Christian?* (Moody, 1957).

Thomas F. O'Dea, *The Mormons* (University of Chicago, 1957) – a good, scholarly survey.

John L. Smith, *Has Mormonism Changed?* (Utah Evangel Press, 1959).

Unity

JAN KAREL
VAN BAALEN

A husband and his wife, physically and financially depressed, followed a hint in an address by a "metaphysical lecturer," Eugene B. Weeks. *"I am a child of God, and therefore do not inherit sickness."* This thought healed Myrtle Fillmore of tuberculosis and, later, her husband, Charles, of a diseased hip. Raised in a Christian environment, they connected it thoroughly with Christian terminology, and then with all-encompassing faith they applied the thought in every direction.

HISTORY

The movement began with debts in the year 1890, but it grew through free will offerings in return for literature and prayers freely distributed. Today its influence spreads around the earth, including Nigeria. Statistics, however, are not available, as the cult prefers (like the Bahá'is) to work silently and pervasively.

In 1891 the name Unity suddenly dawned upon Charles Fillmore. "That's it," he cried. "UNITY! That's the name for our work, the name we've been looking for! The name came right out of the ether, just as the voice of Jesus was heard by Paul alone. No

---

J. K. van Baalen is author of 11 books, among them *The Chaos of Cults and Christianity Versus the Cults.* Minister emeritus of the Christian Reformed Church, he marked his 70th birthday last April and, after the loss of his wife and a son, he wrote *When Hearts Grow Faint,* published by Eerdmans. He holds the B.D. from University of Kampen, the Netherlands, and the Th.M. from Princeton Theological Seminary.

one heard it, but it was as clear to me as though somebody had spoken to me."

Blest with two sons, Rickert the architect-farmer, and Lowell the organizer, the organization has built two centers, the Unity Society of Practical Christianity in Kansas City, Missouri, and the more recent headquarters, the Unity School of Christianity at Lee's Summit, Missouri. They operate "the best vegetarian cafeteria in the world" (though the eating of meat is not strictly forbidden, and Charles ate fish in his later years), they own huge printing presses and a powerful broadcasting station, they distribute freely and sell tons of books and pamphlets, and they have year-round training classes and education for "Unity ministry." In 1910 they organized "The Silent 70," who distribute free literature including testimonials concerning cures effected. Also there is "The Silent Unity," 100 workers who engage in 24-hour prayer in answer to thousands of telegrams, letters, and telephone calls requesting intercession for health, solution of marital problems, success upon business ventures, and so on. Prayer is as effective when sent up by others as when it is personally offered, since the ones requesting prayer thereby show a great faith.

At first the cult was loosely identified with Christian Science and New Thought (the magazine was called *Modern Thought,* then *Christian Science Thought,* later *Unity*). In 1922 the Fillmores withdrew once for all from the INTA (International New Thought Alliance). Unity has developed somewhat less materialistically than New Thought, and less egocentrically than Christian Science.

Some evangelical ministers, Roman Catholic priests, and rabbis leave Unity tracts in hospitals. These tracts are often phrased so that when read against a Christian background they can be helpful. But they are decidedly harmful when the underlying anti-Christian philosophy is not detected and Unity's gross allegorizing of Scripture is swallowed.

Unity ministers have recently organized many churches, first known as Unity Centers, now also as Unity Church of Truth. More conscious of their independent organization, these ministers broadcast a "Unity Viewpoint" and "At the Silent Unity Prayer Hour." Great stress is laid upon "praying with Silent Unity at 11 o'clock every morning." In Missouri all work stops several times daily for prayer, and great value is ascribed to hearing the Lord's Prayer from a tape recording in Charles Fillmore's own voice (he died in July, 1948, at the age of 94). Local churches, however, remain bound to Unity headquarters by an Annual Conference.

WHAT UNITY TEACHES

Unity began with an emphasis on healing from bodily disease. It is not to be confused with Faith Healing which looks to a transcendent God in the name of the divine-human Saviour Jesus Christ. Unity shares with the latter the mistake of believing it is not in the will of God for anyone to be ill and that all failure to be healed is due to lack of faith. But Unity surpasses in error the theory of Faith Healing, for it does not look toward "The Lord thy Healer" of Scripture but to a divine principle within man himself. It is, like New Thought and Eddyism, a mind-healing cult. Charles Fillmore wrote in *Modern Thought*: "These columns are open to teachers and healers who advocate and practice Pure Mind-Healing only. . . . Not that we condemn any system, but . . . we find by experience that concentration is necessary to success and we wish to confine these pages to that specific doctrine, and Holy Ghost power, taught and demonstrated by Jesus Christ" (*The Story of Unity,* p. 57).

The Fillmores never denied the reality of matter, sickness, and death, as did Mrs. Eddy, but they asserted that existing evil can be removed by mind, truth, thought. Thus it becomes clear why they developed a less illogical type of mind-healing than did Christian Science, and why they abandoned the name of Christian Science Thought. Mrs. Eddy both denies the reality of evil and posits it as a product of Mortal Mind, an entity for which there is really no room in a system that asserts that God is All, and All is Good. Unity admits the reality of evil, but it asserts that God, Principle, Truth is more powerful than evil and therefore is able to drive evil out physically, economically, in fact completely from human existence.

The Fillmores assert that evil is the product of wrong thought, to be abolished by right thinking (*Story,* p. 60). Most telling for the claims of the theory is the title of Charles Fillmore's last book, *Atom-Smashing Power of Mind.* All matter is full of energy. When released, a drop of water may blow up a 10-story building. Life is based upon the interaction between the various electrical units of the universe. Science tells about these units, but only the spiritually-developed man can understand them. Faith rouses man's physical cells to expectancy and results take place.

This cure-all of the mind operates in every sphere. All causes lie in the mental man. The physician thinks that disease germs "are an integral part of the natural world; the metaphysician sees disease germs as the manifested results of anger, revenge, jealousy, fear, impurity, and many other mind activities. . . . To attain prosperity, think about prosperity, industry, and efficiency (*ibid,* pp. 99, 104).

EVALUATION

The emphasis upon "mind over matter" is good. Every intelligent person knows that emotion (spiritual) may cause blushing or pallor (physical); that anger, hatred, revenge, fear do cause headaches, angina pectoris, heart attacks, neuroses, insanity. Physicians and pastors realize that this territory of knowledge has only been partly explored. Many sicknesses do result from wrong thinking, but germs do not, though depressing thoughts lower physical resistance to germs.

Our churches would be in better condition if Christians would consult as freely with the indwelling Holy Spirit as Unity devotees do with their indwelling God. In the case of Christianity, the transcendent Holy Spirit does a regenerating and sanctifying work within us, while in Unity a man's own divine spirit, mind, or energy is supposed to perform such a work.

The basic error of Unity, therefore, which it shares with Christian Science, New Thought, Theosophy, and Rosicrucianism, is its pantheism. Man, according to biblical teaching, is not divine. His mind is created. But H. E. Cady states that "though to the awakened mind it may seem that it is more money as money, or more goods that he wants, it is nevertheless, more of good (God) that he craves; for all is God" (*Lessons in Truth*, p. 87). Unity literature is full of pantheism. We must "find the Christ in us." "God is all." "God is principle." Truth resides in all men regardless of their racial or religious background. "Keep ever in mind that each living person in all God's universe is a radiating center of the same perfect One." By mere concentrated thought upon a person, we can awake in him the sense of divinity (Cady, *ibid.*, p. 135).

Being sheer pantheism, Unity denies the guilt of sin. Sin is a transgression of the law, to be eliminated by a return to law. And man, being mentally divine, is able to do this. This declaration is a radical denial of Romans 8:7, "The mind of the flesh is enmity against God."

Since sin entails no guilt, there is no sentence of death as "the wages of sin" (Rom. 6:23). Fillmore expected almost to the end that he would not die; finally he thought he was to live on in an astral body (cf. Theosophy) and continue in a reincarnation. There can be no atonement, no propitiation, no penalty paid for sin by Jesus Christ. We need only to learn about "at-one-ment" with God through a pantheistic "inflow" of spirit or energy.

Unity resents the biblical teaching that sickness and death may be a punishment sent by a just and holy God (cf. Miriam's and Gehazi's leprosy, Num. 12:10, II Kings 5:27; Jehoram's enteritis, II Chron. 21:18; the death of David's child, II Sam. 12:8; the death of Ananias, Acts 5).

Unity fails to understand that adversity may be a Godsend and affliction may lead to spiritual advantage: Job said, "Now mine eye seeth thee"; the psalmist gave thanks, "It is good for me that I have been afflicted"; Paul wrote, "I take pleasure in weaknesses"; and even Jesus "learned obedience by the things which he suffered."

Unity reduces God to a Do-gooder, not One to be served and glorified but a principle to serve and to obey the human will. His funds are inexhaustible and at our disposal because we all are fundamentally divine and good. "The Lord is my banker; my credit is good. He maketh me to lie down in the consciousness of omnipotent abundance; He giveth me the key to His strong-box . . . and I shall do business in the name of the Lord forever" (Fillmore). Jesus Christ becomes the "Way-shower," our personified ideal. Christianity becomes a religion of getting on without crossbearing.

Like Swedenborgianism, Unity allegorizes Scripture, declaring it to be parable where it is clearly written as historic incident. Genesis 1-2 "is a symbolic story of the work of the higher realms of mind under divine law" (*Atom*, p. 12). The tabernacle and the temple are symbols of man's body, "the real meeting place of Jehovah" (*ibid.*, p. 80). The story of the fall is symbolism (*Christian Healing*, p. 21). Jesus' transfiguration is an allegory demonstrating the universal possibility of attainment or realization (*Atom*, p. 152). The apostles symbolize "a higher expression of the faculties." Simon Peter is hearing and faith. John is feeling and love joined (*Christian Healing*, p. 73). King Herod represents the ego in the outer sense consciousness. Jesus represents God's idea of man in expression; Christ is that idea in the absolute (*Unity*, Vol. 72, No. 1).

As to Unity's healings, many of them are genuine. Let us appreciate the emphasis of mind over matter. Other healings are not. Charles Fillmore remained a cripple. Unity judges only by the patient's own testimony and refuses to submit to a physician's diagnosis. In view of the vehemently anti-Christian doctrine of Unity, we should not forget that St. Paul ascribes to Satan the power of doing "lying wonders" through his human agents (II Thess. 2:9). Satan is never more dangerous than when he walks in velvet slippers.

SELECTION OF BOOKS FOR STUDY

Pamphlets for study are: *Help for Alcoholics; The Master's Ten Laws for Human Relations; As You Tithe So You Prosper; Maternity Lessons; A Ten-Point Creed for Teen-Age Drivers; Wherever You Are God is Near; What Unity Teaches; Training School Prospectus* (Unity School of Christianity, Lee's Summit, Missouri). The standard publications by The Silent 70 are: *Unity, Daily Word, Weekly Unity, Good Business, You, Wee Wisdom.* Books published by Unity School of Christianity (Lee's Summit, Missouri) are as follows:

Charles Fillmore, *Christian Healing* (1909, 1957).

Charles Fillmore, *Atom-Smashing Power of Mind* (1949, 1957).

James Dillet Freeman, *The Story of Unity* (1954).

H. Emilie Cady, *Lessons in Truth* (1958).

Marcus Bach, *They Have Found a Faith* (Bobbs-Merrill, 1946).

Charles S. Braden, *These Also Believe* (Macmillan, 1949).

Paul Tournier, *A Doctor's Case-book in the Light of the Bible* (Harper, 1960).

J. K. van Baalen, *When Hearts Grow Faint,* Instructions on How to Live a Life of Joy (Eerdmans, 1960).

J. K. van Baalen, *The Chaos of Cults* (third edition, Eerdmans, 1960).

Seventh-day Adventism

WALTER R. MARTIN

From its very inception in the wake of the defunct Millerite Movement, the Seventh-day Adventist Church has been a center of controversy. Even today, over a century later, it is virtually impossible for evangelical Christians to maintain neutrality in the debate stirred by the movement.

HISTORICAL BACKGROUND

William Miller, a Baptist minister, of Low Hampton, New York, popularized the preaching of the second advent of Christ in the early part of the nineteenth century and predicted it would take place in 1843. When Miller's calculation was proved false, after a second guess, October 22, 1844, he manfully admitted his error and dissociated himself from the movement. Others, however, were not of Miller's persuasion and taught instead that Christ did return in 1844, not to the earthly sanctuary but to the "heavenly sanctuary." This concept grew among those desirous of salvaging not only their reputations as Bible students but their very allegiance to "Adventism" as a special "Latter Day message" prior to the glorious appearing of Christ.

Walter R. Martin is Director of the Christian Research Institute and Editor of *Religious Research Digest,* which is devoted to a biblical appraisal of the major cults. An ordained Baptist minister, he holds the B.A. and B.R.E. degrees from Shelton College and the M.A. from New York University where he is a doctoral candidate. He has authored several books among which are *The Rise of the Cults, The Christian and the Cults* and *The Truth about Seventh-day Adventism.*

This group soon joined with two other disillusioned segments of the now rapidly disintegrating Millerite Movement. One emphasized the Seventh day sabbath and the other endorsed the so-called "Spirit of Prophecy" as allegedly revealed in the life and ministry of Ellen G. White.

Under the leadership of Mrs. White, almost a supernatural figure by Adventist standards, her husband James, Joseph Bates, a retired sea captain, and Hiram Edson whose revelation of the "heavenly sanctuary truth" appropriately occurred in a cornfield, Seventh-day Adventism as a denomination was born.

The Adventists succeeded almost immediately in isolating themselves from fellowship with other Christian groups by enunciating their "special truths" (the sabbath, the heavenly sanctuary, the investigative judgment, and the spirit of prophecy) and by condemning those who opposed their views as "Babylon," future recipients of the "mark of the beast" (Rev. 13:16-18). In addition, they vigorously preached premillennial Adventism in a largely a-millennial theological climate and engaged in numerous debates aimed chiefly at promoting their "sabbath truth." These developments hardly made for good public relations or understanding between Adventists and their fellow Christians. But as the Seventh-day Adventist Church grew it gradually rectified a large number of these inconsistencies through a program Ellen White herself implemented and supported.

SCOPE OF THE MOVEMENT

Today the Seventh-day Adventist Church numbers in excess of 1,155,000 adult baptized members, while it has over 1,500,000 Sabbath School members throughout the world. Adventists have some 6,000 ordained ministers and more than 3,300 licensed ministers. They operate 44 publishing houses producing literature in over 200 languages; they preach and teach in about 800 languages and dialects. They publish 385 periodicals and more than 60 new books yearly and have enrolled more than 3,000,000 persons in their Bible study courses offered over the radio. Their "Voice of Prophecy" radio program is heard on 860 stations and reaches people in some 65 languages. "Faith for Today," their official television program is heard on 153 stations in the United States as well as many stations abroad. The *Signs of the Times* and *These Times*, their largest missionary magazines, have a combined circulation of 400,000 copies a month.

In the field of individual church support, the Seventh-day Adventists contributed during 1958 more than $83,000,000 for their church work at home and abroad, while the literature sales of the denomination amounted to $22,000,000. They contributed on the average of over $216 per person. In addition the Adventists maintain 220 medical units employing over 420 doctors in 107 sanitariums and hospitals with 114 clinics and dispensaries. They have numerous medical launches and welfare projects in areas around the globe.

It is interesting to note by way of contrast that the average per capita contribution for all denominations in the United States is $48.81! Though still a relatively small denomination, the Adventists claim to have more missionaries active on foreign fields than any Protestant body except the Methodists who have a little over 1500; the Adventists have in excess of 1400. The total Adventist working force is more than 46,000 persons, a total of 12,500 churches organized in the 425 conferences and union conferences. The Adventist school system, comprising 5,216 schools and colleges, employs more than 12,000 teachers. Approximately

275,000 are attending their schools.

The growth of the denomination obviously has been rapid and the zeal of its devotees enviable. With its rigid adherence to the basic principles of the Christian Gospel and its strict demand for a "separated" life (abstinence from tobacco, alcohol, worldly amusements and certain articles of diet), Seventh-day Adventism has a definite appeal to a considerable segment of our populace. Both in the United States and abroad it continues to grow in numbers, in missionary influence and in public status.

BASIC THEOLOGY

The basic theological structure of Seventh-day Adventism is essentially orthodox. The movement holds to the inspiration of Scripture, the Christian doctrines of the Trinity, Deity of Christ, Virgin Birth, Vicarious Atonement, Bodily Resurrection, and Second Advent of our Lord. Despite some apparent tendencies toward legalism (emphasis upon the decalogue, particularly the sixth commandment, and abstinence from foods prohibited under the Mosaic legislation) Adventists in their evangelical efforts and general church worship teach that salvation is by grace alone through faith in Jesus Christ. For them observance of the law of God is one of the good works that are a by-product of such a redemption (Eph. 2:8-10). After a thorough examination of the theology of Seventh-day Adventism and a wide acquaintance with its leadership, churches, and educational institutions in the United States and on the world mission field, this writer is convinced that it is essentially a Christian denomination, but that in the over-all perspective its theology must be viewed as more heterodox than orthodox, and that its practices in not a few instances might rightly be termed Divisive.

HETERODOX DOCTRINE

Historic Christianity differs from the theology of Seventh-day Adventism in the following major ways:

1. Adventism teaches that the Seventh-day Sabbath is obligatory on all Christians as a mark of "true obedience" to the Lord. This has never been the historic position of the Christian Church since the days of the Apostles. Not one line in the New Testament after the resurrection of our Lord indicates that there is to be concern about the keeping of days. Romans 14 is explicit in stating that believers are not to judge each other in the matter of the observation of days or dietetic prohibitions. Adventists are guilty of violating this principle since they repeatedly insist upon Sabbath observance for those who have no conviction on this question. Paul instructs the Church to "let every man be fully persuaded in his own mind." In Colossians, chapter 2, the apostle charges the Church not to be enslaved to the regulation of feast days, new moons and sabbaths; and in Galatians, historically written against legalism, he is disturbed because of their concern about the observance of "days." Adventists would do well to take these portions of Scripture more seriously rather than compile voluminous quotations from the Old Testament and the New Testament prior to the Resurrection to obscure the obvious intent of the Apostolic message.

2. The theology of Adventism is also deficient because of the authoritative status it assigns to its own extra-biblical literature. This it does by utilizing the writings of Ellen G. White who allegedly possessed "the gift of prophecy." Though I am convinced that Seventh-day Adventists do not worship or believe in the infallibility of Mrs. White's counsels, it is a disturbing sight to attend their quadrennial session and

hear the speakers monotonously "buttress" the clear teaching of the Scriptures by various quotations from the writings of Mrs. White. We need not believe that Mrs. White's "visions" were of the devil in order to reject them.

3. One doctrine peculiar to Seventh-day Adventism is that of the so-called "heavenly sanctuary and the investigative judgment." This view maintains that Christ entered into the "second phase" of his heavenly ministry in 1844, a view which is nothing more than a projection of the Hiram Edson "vision" redefined and spiritualized to escape the obvious deficiencies of the earlier literalistic view. In Edson's view, fully developed by O. R. L. Crosier and endorsed by Ellen G. White, Christ then actually passed from the first apartment of the sanctuary in heaven into the second apartment. This, however, is flatly contradicted by the book of Hebrews which declares that "he entered once into the holy place [first and second apartments, if you will], having obtained eternal redemption for us" (Heb. 9:12). Since the Book of Hebrews was written well before 1844, our Lord could hardly be construed as waiting for eighteen centuries to elapse before entering the "second apartment." In their book *Questions on Doctrine,* the Adventists have entered a footnote on page 385 which mentions the exegesis of the previously quoted passage in Hebrews and indicates their awareness of the linguistic difficulty of supporting the old Edson-Crosier-White dogma.

The "investigative judgment" theory holds that there is a judgment going on in heaven now in which the cases of those who believe on Christ here on earth are being reviewed to determine whether they are "worthy" of eternal life. This view was rejected by James White himself far more eloquently than I can present a refutation. One regrets that under the pressure of his wife's "visions" and the circumstances which surrounded him at a later date he retracted what is an almost flawless refutation of the position endorsed by the Adventist denomination. We might add that any careful reading of John 5:24 would indicate that the Christian has already passed from death to life and shall never come under judgment for his eternal destiny, since Christ bore that judgment fully upon the Cross (Col. 2:14). We shall of course appear before the judgment seat of Christ for those deeds done in the body; but this is a judgment of rewards, as Scripture clearly indicates, not of eternal destiny. The "investigative judgment" is a modified Arminian device for stimulating obedience in the life of Adventists—obedience that ought to be motivated by the love of the Lord Jesus Christ and overwhelming gratitude for his full and free salvation.

CONDITIONAL IMMORTALITY

Finally, Adventism is apparently unalterably committed to the doctrine of conditional immortality. Such a view which does away with the doctrine of hell and eternal conscious punishment of the lost has been espoused by not a few theologians and laymen through the centuries, but 98 per cent of the Christian Church has chosen to follow the doctrine of the Apostles and of our Lord, who taught the existence of conscious punishment of an eternal duration in terms few could fail to understand (Matt. 25:41, 46).

These and other views, not to mention the disconcerting Adventist habit of proselytizing Christian converts and failing to identify themselves properly when conducting large campaigns, are a constant source of misunderstanding between Adventists and their fellow Christians. They are also a strong deterrent to a full and effective fellowship with Seventh-day Adventists in the minds of some.

CHRISTIAN FELLOWSHIP

That fellowship of Christians is commanded by Jesus Christ and the Apostles none can fairly deny, but that its implementation is made difficult by the divisive activities of certain members of the "Body" no one can challenge. Until Seventh-day Adventists and certain of their overly antagonistic detractors come to terms with the great biblical command of love between brethren and discipline within the Church, which is his Body, friction will continue and will make full realization of fellowship extremely difficult. That Adventists should be recognized as Christians and that fellowship should be extended to them we do not deny. They are a Christian denomination rather than an anti-Christian cult. But they have been divisive in their activities and legalistic in their demand that they be recognized as the enunciators of "special truths" unknown to the Church as a whole for almost two thousand years. This we most emphatically reject. We must oppose those sections of their theology which are contrary to the historic Christian message, but we must do so by speaking the truth in love.

SELECTION OF BOOKS FOR STUDY

It is difficult to recommend authoritative sources dealing with the history and doctrines of Seventh-day Adventism because so much of the literature is deeply prejudiced and lacks documentation and Christian charity. The following works, however, do give Adventism a reasonably objective consideration and are generally reliable in the area of apologetics.

Dictionary of American Biography, vol. 12, Article on William Miller.

W. Fletcher, *Reasons for My Faith* (William Brooks and Company, Ltd., Sydney, Australia).

Norman C. Deck, *The Lord's Day or the Sabbath* (Bridge Printery Ltd., Sydney, Australia).

F. E. Mayer, *The Religious Bodies of America* (Concordia).

Questions on Doctrine (Review and Herald, Takoma Park, 1957).

Walter R. Martin, *The Truth About Seventh Day Adventism* (Zondervan, 1960).

Dudley M. Canright, *Seventh Day Adventism Renounced* (B. C. Goodpasture, Nashville, Tennessee).

Horton Davies, *Christian Deviations* (Philosophical Library, New York).

J. Oswald Sanders and J. Stafford Wright, *Some Modern Religions* (Inter-Varsity Press, England).

John Gerstner, *Theology of the Major Sects* (Baker, 1960).

J. K. van Baalen, *The Chaos of Cults* (Eerdmans, 1960).

Harold Lindsell, "What of Seventh-day Adventism?" CHRISTIANITY TODAY (Mar. 31 and Apr. 14, 1958).

Frank H. Yost, "A Seventh-day Adventist Speaks Back," CHRISTIANITY TODAY (July 21, 1958).

Douglas Auchincloss, "Peace With the Adventists," *Time* Magazine (Dec. 31, 1956).

Donald Grey Barnhouse, "Are Seventh-day Adventists Christians?" *Eternity* (Aug., 1956).

Questions on Doctrine | A CLEFT IN SEVENTH-DAY ADVENTISM?

Since the current controversy over the classification of Seventh-day Adventists (denomination or cult?) was first initiated in 1956, one interesting factor in the conflict has gone largely unnoticed. The Adventists apparently have been faced by growing internal tension and division as a result of the publication of their definitive volume, *Questions on Doctrine,* and of Walter Martin's new book, *The Truth About Seventh-day Adventism.*

The rumblings, first beneath the surface, can now be heard audibly in not a few quarters. The fact that there has been a marked change or redefinition of certain facets of Seventh-day

Adventist theology, was pointed out by *The Gathering Call,* published by ex-Seventh-day Adventists. An article entitled "Moving the Landmarks" considers the Adventists' volume, *Questions on Doctrine,* and articles published in *Eternity* magazine by Donald Grey Barnhouse and Walter R. Martin. The editors of the *Call* point out that some of the old Adventist landmarks have been moved, notably the alleged inerrancy of Ellen White, the vicarious nature of the scapegoat translation of Leviticus 16, and the literal interpretation of the Heavenly Sanctuary doctrine. According to *The Gathering Call,* historic adventism stands repudiated in these areas, a charge supplemented by other interesting considerations. A. L. Hudson, former elder in a large Adventist church in Oregon, in company with retired yet powerful Adventist leader Dr. M. L. Andreasen, has spearheaded a move to have those responsible for the publication of *Questions of Doctrine* censured for "misrepresenting the historic position" of the Adventist church. From as far away as Australia and New Zealand letters have reached us concerning the small but apparently vocal segment of Adventism that still wants to brand Sunday keepers with "the mark of the beast," teach a literalistic sanctuary and scapegoat transaction, and hold Ellen White in esteem as an infallible "prophetess." Dr. Andreasen at one time was professor of theology at the Adventists' seminary in Washington, D.C.

Leaders of the Seventh-day Adventist denomination have, however, discounted this faction as unrepresentative of the views of the major constituency of the Church. This affirmation is apparently underscored by the fact that the book, *Questions on Doctrine,* authorized by the General Conference as the denominational position, has had the widest circulation and general approval of the denomination of any volume of recent years. But the fact remains that there is a segment of Seventh-day Adventists vocal and apparently powerful enough to reverse some of the trends originally undertaken in good faith by the leadership of the denomination in 1956.

It is significant to note that *The Signs of the Times* and *These Times,* major Adventist publications, have identified themselves for the first time as publications of the Seventh-day Adventist Church, only to have the identification rescinded and withdrawn from the masthead. Certain publications which allegedly did not represent the position of the denomination are still widely circulated despite the assurance of the leadership of the Seventh-day Adventist denomination that "plans were already operative" to dispense with such inconsistencies in Adventist publishing houses. (Adventist spokesmen assert that, in a sense, each of their publishing houses is autonomous, having its own board of control, and that the reasons for masthead changes lie with the editors.)

Another interesting fact is the Adventist denomination's attitude toward Mr. Martin's book, which leaders endorsed as accurately representing their views. Martin's book was to be stocked by Adventist publishing houses according to commitments made by top Adventist officials. Authorization to place his book on sale was not forthcoming, however, despite the fact that two non-critical non-Adventist publications were accepted for distribution. (Adventist spokesmen point out that their book and Bible houses are set up as retail outlets for their own publishing houses, and only occasionally is the sale of outside books authorized. "Martin's book sets forth our views accurately," said one leader, "but that's only half the story. It also attempts to expose as fallacious the most distinctive of these views. Why should a religious body promote books that seek to refute these teachings?")

The cleft in Seventh-day Adventism seems, however, to be deeper than appears on the surface. Some Seventh-day Adventist officials seem not to welcome any investigation of their views due to their divergence from what the church maintains as its true position.

One thing, however, is certain. Certain elements in the theology of Seventh-day Adventism are in flux; some of the old landmarks have apparently been moved; and some old errors have been or are being rectified. Perhaps the Adventist denomination would be wiser to admit these faults publicly. By so doing they would probably escape the growing conviction in some circles that they cannot control irresponsible, unrepresentative elements within the church, and are content to remain silent where decisive action would settle the issue. Such action would promote stronger ties of fellowship and respect for the integrity of Adventism among Christians of other denominations.

Jehovah's Witnesses

WILBUR M. SMITH

The latest of the major cults arising and exercising much influence in our country is today known as Jehovah's Witnesses—a cult which will soon count itself to be 100 years old, though its earlier days are strangely passed by in its more recent literature. Although this cult has always produced an enormous literature (one periodical has 3 million circulation a week) and its members are zealous in the promotion of beliefs and the circulation of books and magazines, it may be surprising that, according to their own statistics, they do not have today in this country—though approaching the century mark—more than one quarter of a million followers.

STRANGE TITLE

The very name Jehovah's Witnesses, which has been the organization's official title for the last 30 years, indicates somewhat the basic tenets of the group. "Jehovah's Witnesses" is a title based upon a phrase found three times in a central passage in one book of the Bible, namely, Isaiah 43:10,12, and 44:8, in which the Lord says, "Ye are my witnesses, saith Jehovah, and my servant whom I have chosen." This title deserves more careful study than it has received. In the first place, the words of the Lord were spoken to the people of

---

Wilbur M. Smith is Professor of English Bible in Fuller Theological Seminary and Editor of *Peloubet's Select Notes on the International Sunday School Lessons.* He is the author of many books, including *The Supernaturalness of Christ, Therefore Stand!*, and recently, *A Treasury of Books for Bible Study.*

Israel. In these two chapters of Isaiah, the Lord again and again identifies the people to whom he is speaking as Israel, and sometimes calls them by the name of Jacob, the father of the 12 tribes from which Israel developed. God is speaking as "the king of Israel" (44:6). Whatever else Jehovah's Witnesses may say, they would not dare to claim that 2,500 years ago, God, speaking through Isaiah, was referring to this cult when he used the phrase, "my servant whom I have chosen," and yet it is to these "chosen" people that God assigns this particular type of witnessing. The word here translated *witness* in its various forms is found about 300 times in the Old Testament. Sometimes it is David who is the witness (Isa. 55:4); we read that God has established a testimony in Jacob (Ps. 78:5), or in Joseph (Ps. 81:5). Over 150 times the word is used in reference to the Tabernacle as "the Tabernacle of testimony." Often it is used in reference to the word of God, as "Thy testimonies are very sure" (Ps. 93:5), and in the 119th Psalm.

This word *witness* holds great importance in the New Testament Scriptures. Christians are repeatedly exhorted and commanded to be witnesses, but *never once* are they referred to in the New Testament as "Jehovah's Witnesses." It is essential, I think, to enlarge upon the evidence here. The Holy Spirit has been sent to bear witness of Christ (John 15:26). All Christians are to be witnesses of Christ (John 15:27; Acts 3:15; 5:32; 10:39; and 22:15). The Apostle Peter says that he was a witness "of the sufferings of Christ" (I Pet. 5:1). The Apostles were especially to be the witnesses of Christ's resurrection (Acts 1:22; 2:32; 4:33; 10:41; 13:31). Our Lord just before his ascension told the disciples that they were to be witnesses of the things concerning himself (Luke 24:48; Acts 1:8). Moreover, the Apostle Peter reminds us that it is to Christ that all the prophets bear witness (Acts 10:43), and this includes Isaiah. One verse in the New Testament does indeed contain the phrase "the witness of God." But this is how that phrase is used: ". . . the witness of God is this, that he hath borne witness concerning his Son. He that believeth on the Son of God hath the witness in him: he that believeth not God hath made him a liar; because he hath not believed in the witness that God hath borne concerning his Son. And the witness is this, that God gave unto us eternal life, and this life is in his Son" (I John 5:9-11).

This modern cult, in taking the title of Jehovah's Witnesses, thus identifies itself with a pre-Christian revelation given to Israel, and in so doing it ignores and in fact repudiates all the New Testament passages relating to this matter of witnessing. Because of this fact, we shall not be surprised to find that its literature denies the Godhead of Christ. Its adherents do not preach a gospel of redemption through Christ's precious blood, and they do not bear witness to the resurrection of Christ, because they do not believe that he rose from the dead. As a corollary, the emphasis of Jehovah's Witnesses is on an earthly kingdom, their many places of worship being called Kingdom Hall. It is not wrong to believe in a final earthly Messianic kingdom. But since the advent, death, and resurrection of Jesus Christ this is not the basic message for the redeemed.

Jehovah's witnesses did not always fear this name. From the beginning of Pastor Russell's work in 1872 and for about 12 years, they lacked a specific name. In 1884, they adopted the name of Zion's Watchtower Society (note again the Old Testament emphasis in the word Zion). In 1909 they were known as The People's Pulpit Association, although they are silent about this in their own contemporary literature. In 1914 they took the widely-used name, The International Bible

Students' Association. Not until 1931, under the leadership of Judge Rutherford, did they adopt the title used today, Jehovah's Witnesses, a title which Pastor Russell never used nor intended to use. One conclusion at least must be drawn. For 60 years this group was without the title which they now believe has been divinely given to them.

Moreover, in a very mysterious way they seem by their silence to be repudiating the work and teachings of their earlier leaders, both generally and specifically. For example, Pastor Russell put a great deal of emphasis on the prophetic teachings of the great pyramids of Egypt, but Judge Rutherford repudiated this in the cult's later official publications (see *The Watchtower and Herald of Christ's Presence,* Vol. 49, 1928, pp. 339-345, and 355-361). Christian Scientists are unwaveringly loyal to the writings of Mary Baker Eddy, their founder. But not so Jehovah's Witnesses. Toward the end of Judge Rutherford's leadership (he died in 1942), the writings of Pastor Russell were scarcely referred to, and for the last 20 years, they have not officially been distributed. The same thing has happened to the writings of Judge Rutherford. One cannot find the name of Pastor Russell as an author in the United States catalogue after 1935, and one cannot find the name of Judge Rutherford as an author in the same exhaustive work after 1944! This emphasizes one undeniable fact that the early teachings of the leaders, at least in part, are now given up, and that only the more recent literature, which by the way is always anonymous, is to be considered official and worthy of confidence for this generation.

As one delves into the literature, one will find many reasons why the earlier writings, of which millions of copies, once distributed, should no longer be recognized as authoritative. Take for example the constant shifting of dates from the end of this age, the coming of antichrist, and so on. In 1889 Pastor Russell wrote concerning the Gentiles: "The full end of their lease of dominion will be reached in 1914, and that date will be the farthest limit of the rule of imperfect men" (*Studies in the Scriptures,* Vol. 2, pp. 76 f). This statement was repeated frequently, even after 1914 had passed. Judge Rutherford then set 1925 to be an epochal year in world government, but this likewise proved incorrect. Although the World War took place in 1914—which was hardly what Pastor Russell promised—he then declared that Christ did return to earth in 1914, expelled Satan from heaven, and proceeded to overthrow Satan's organization and establish the theocratic millennial kingdom (see *The Kingdom is at Hand,* pp. 300 ff.). The fearful events that we have witnessed on earth since 1914 do not bear testimony to any theory that Satan's organization is now being overthrown! In fact, in the 1923 edition of *Studies in the Scriptures,* the phrase "before 1914" is now changed to "very soon after 1914." While they teach that Christ's second advent has already occurred, for which there is no evidence, they at the same time repudiate the clear teaching of the New Testament concerning this event. Judge Rutherford insisted that "we should not expect the Lord's second coming to be in a body visible to human eyes" (*The Harp of God,* p. 225).

SOME UNSAVORY FACTORS

Hundreds of pages have been written about the falsehoods, indiscretions, and questionable practices of Pastor Russell, and it is only necessary to recall these briefly. Pastor Russell's wife, whom he married in 1879, and who in the early years was a devoted follower of her husband's teachings, felt compelled to separate from him in 1897, and brought suit for divorce in 1913.

The divorce was won, and, though the verdict was constantly appealed, yet five different times the courts sustained the original verdict. The sordid story of the Egyptian wheat need not be considered here. Pastor Russell faced numerous court trials, both in our country and Canada. While he was a man of great energy and organizing ability, with some facility in clearly expressing his views on the Scriptures, the subjects of holiness, of conflict with evil in the soul, of surrender to the leading and dominion of the Holy Spirit, find no emphasis in his literature nor in the cult's teaching.

When we come to the doctrinal beliefs of Jehovah's Witnesses, we face the most tragic aspect of the entire movement. Underlying all its other teaching is the fact that Jehovah's Witnesses are anti-Trinitarian, and in repudiating the doctrine of the Trinity they remove themselves beyond the pale of the Christian Church. Specifically they say that "This One was not Jehovah God. . . . He was a mighty one, although not almighty as Jehovah God is. . . . He was *a* God, but not the almighty God" (*The Kingdom at Hand,* pp. 34 f; also *Reconciliation,* p. 111). In fact, they have the abominable idea that God had two sons, the Logos, to be identified with Christ, and Lucifer, the son of the Morning who, ultimately by his fall, became the devil. Not only do they repudiate the deity of Christ but they deny the personality of the Holy Spirit. "The Holy Spirit is not a person and is, therefore, not one of the Trinity" (*Reconciliation,* p. 114).

Furthermore, they hold the view that Christ was not crucified, but was impaled on a tree, and that the Cross is a pagan symbol, a phallic emblem. They insist that at Christ's death, his human body somehow evaporated or God buried it somewhere unknown to anyone. Christ the Man has been dead all these centuries, and the one who was raised from the dead was not the human Christ but an invisible spirit, and the body in which he revealed himself to the disciples after his death was not the body in which he died.

These radical departures from the clear teachings of Scripture are not simply new or fantastic interpretations of what may be called "debatable areas" of biblical teaching; they are repudiations of the great central truths of the Christian faith! To deny these truths is to excommunicate oneself from the true Body of Christ, the deity of Jesus Christ, his redeeming work accomplished on the Cross, his bodily resurrection, the person and work of the Holy Spirit, a true love for the brethren, the certainty of a judgment to come, and the absolute oneness of *all* believers in Christ, whatever be their particular denominational adherence. Jehovah's Witnesses have a commendable enthusiasm in propagating their views, but they proclaim a false religion.

BITTER REPUDIATION OF CHRISTIANS

One of the most deplorable features of the whole movement, from the very beginning of Pastor Russell's teachings, is the constant and abusive verbal attack on clergy and Christians. They have been called the tools of Satan, the incarnation of anti-Christ, Haman, and so on. These anti-Church fanatics even go so far as to make Ezekiel 22:26-29 apply to clergymen of the Church today. The Church is called the great enemy of God, and they frankly say they must hate God's enemies. The Church is likened to the Moabites whenever it opposes Jehovah's Witnesses. One quotation from Judge Rutherford will suffice: "Organized Christianity is hypocritical and selfish in the extreme. There is no real love amongst the people who make up that crowd. The entire crowd is against Jehovah"(*Preparation,* p. 318). How wicked for a group not yet 100 years old to designate as servants of Satan, deceivers, and liars, thousands of faithful ministers and missionaries who have lived godly lives in this century and in others, winning souls, comforting the bereaved, bringing hope to the hopeless, and preaching the Gospel that has set millions free from the power of sin.

If such fantastic beliefs are proclaimed by Jehovah's Witnesses, if the cult's early days were overshadowed by the unethical experiences of Pastor Russell who alienated great numbers of his followers, how then can one account for the multitudes won to its fold? For one thing, the movement claims to be exclusively biblical, and many people still look upon the Bible as the Word of God, but lack the power to discern the false from the true, would be drawn to a group that talks so much about the Bible. Secondly, some people like to think that they belong to an exclusive group, such as "the 144,000," especially if they are persecuted for it, as many of the Jehovah's Witnesses have been. They therefore think that they are the specially elect of God, and this appeals to their pride. Thirdly, they are drawn and held by the very zeal of the movement. They are told to distribute periodicals, rap at the doors of neighbors, take on missionary activities, and promote the teachings of their cult with all the vigor they have. Finally, many people need someone to address them with absolute authority. They need an authoritarian teaching and such they find in Watch Tower literature.

I do not want to say anything disparaging concerning the persons found in this group. But for the most part (and here they differ from Christian Scientists) it must be said that they are rather uneducated. They are almost afraid of education. Sunday Schools are scarce among them. They have not founded educational institutions worthy of accreditation. In fact, they have never produced one volume of biblical interpretation worthy of notice in the progressive development of biblical interpretation in modern times.

SELECTION OF BOOKS FOR STUDY

Herbert Hewitt Stroup, *The Jehovah's Witnesses* (Columbia University Press, 1945) – a thoroughly documented work by one who lived at various headquarters of this group to obtain authentic data.

Milton Stacey Czatt, *The International Bible Students, Jehovah's Witnesses* (Yale Studies on Religion, No. 4, New Haven, 1933) – a careful study of sources.

Royston Pike, *Jehovah's Witnesses* (Watts & Co., London, 1954).

Bruce M. Metzger, "The Jehovah's Witnesses and Jesus Christ. A Biblical and Theological Appraisal" (Originally an article in *Theology Today*, Apr., 1953, now available in pamphlet form, from the Theological Book Agency, Princeton, New Jersey) – an unanswerable indictment of the heresies of this sect regarding the Person of Christ by an outstanding New Testament scholar.

W. J. Schnell, *Thirty Years a Watchtower Slave* (Baker Book House, 1956).

Walter R. Martin and Norman H. Klann, *Jehovah of the Watchtower* (Zondervan, 1953) – valuable discussion of and reply to the denial of the Trinity, with full bibliography of Judge Rutherford's writings.

Spiritualism

PETER FINGESTEN

Spiritualism, which had its heyday in the latter half of the nineteenth century, is having a surprising revival in North America. Hundreds of so-called spiritualist churches regularly engage in healing sessions, led by mystics who claim to transmit "spirit messages." Scores of summer camps implement church programs. Publications such as *Psychic Observer* and *Tomorrow* work hand-in-hand with the American Society for Psychic Research, promoting "scientific proof" of the reality of psychic phenomena. In March, 1956, a group of American ministers, missionaries, and lay leaders organized the Spiritual Frontiers Fellowship, patterned after the British Churches Fellowship for Psychical Research, "to sponsor, explore and interpret the growing interest in psychic phenomena and mystical experience within the church, wherever these experiences relate to effective prayer, spiritual healing, and personal survival." It claims Christian origin and interfaith scope.

Focal point of spiritualism is the séance, ostensible counterpart of a religious service, led by a medium, an individual "gifted" with psychic powers. The medium lapses into a trance which supposedly enables him to contact spiritual forces and to act as speaking intermediary between these forces and other participants in the séance.

Peter Fingesten is Associate Professor of Art at Pace College, New York City. He is the author of the book, *East Is East,* published by Muhlenberg Press in 1956, and has written numerous articles on art and religion for scholarly magazines.

Nineteenth-century pioneers of spiritualism like Conan Doyle, with his photographs of ectoplasm, Oliver Lodge and Flammarion had almost faded from memory when mediums like Eileen Garrett, Edgar Cayce, Alice A. Bailey and Arthur Ford revived it. Today spiritualism surrounds itself with a scientific aura and takes advantage of the widespread interest in parapsychology, or ESP (extra-sensory perception).

In *Parapsychology,* Dr. J. B. Rhine, leading American scholar in this field, cautiously wrote: "It should from the very beginning be made clear that the phenomena with which parapsychology deals are all, without exception, events of nature. In other words, the field of problems belongs entirely to *natural science.*" But in a subsequent paper, "What Next in Parapsychology?," which Dr. Rhine contributed to Eileen Garrett's anthology *Beyond the Five Senses,* he not only contradicts this statement but attempts (a mistake many others have made before him) to explain religion scientifically. "Religion is, of course, the most immediate area of application for parapsychology. Defined as the investigation of non-physical operations in nature and the principles governing them, parapsychology would have to lay claim to many of the more fundamental problems of religion." If this were true, then the spiritual experiences of the prophets and apostles would have been nothing more than early instances of ESP. However, the contrast between modern parapsychology experiments and the insights of eminent Christians would strongly militate against this claim.

To explain religion simply in terms of ESP is to do a disservice to both. ESP is not synonymous with religious-spiritual phenomena such as the visions experienced by biblical figures. There is a great temptation to explain spiritual phenomena scientifically, but man has no scientific tools to investigate supernatural phenomena.

Dr. Rhine concedes that ESP has floundered in its attempt to solve the paramount question of the survival of the soul. "The investigation of the survival question," he says, "has already been a prominent part of parapsychology's history. For a period of fifty years, extending from the eighties into the twenties, it almost eclipsed and excluded every other interest in the field. Nor was the enthusiasm and activity that was generated entirely emotional and uncritical. Some of the ablest scholars of the times were active in the guidance, conduct and interpretation of the studies that were made to focus the issue and establish a conclusion. Eventually, however, with the development of increased emphasis on the necessary precautions, the status of the survival hypothesis became more and more uncertain, and the issue remained inconclusive. Decision on the question had to be left a matter of individual choice and not the necessary result of conclusive scientific proof." This leaves the question exactly where it has always been. Baron Schrenck-Notzing, the great German pioneer of parapsychology, did not fall into this trap but steered clear of religious problems. "The soul is like a bubble upon the ocean," he observed. "Bubbles appear and reappear. Who can say that it is the same bubble? I am not a spiritualist. I am a Parapsychologist." ESP does not deal with spiritual forces in the traditional religious sense, but seeks to deal with human forces shrouded in mystery.

One must be careful, moreover, to distinguish both ESP and spiritualism from authentic religious experiences. So-called psychic phenomena and religious experiences are two different categories, the former is based on human probing, the latter on God's saving revelation in Jesus Christ.

The term "spiritual experience" is used to cover a wide variety of phenomena. There is a striking contrast between the experiences of men who received the biblical revelation and those of modern seekers after psychic "messages." The prophets and apostles were chosen — they did not choose. They did not try to crash the uncharted realms of the infinite with the help of mediums or ouija boards, nor did "spirit guides" reveal to them the fate of an Uncle Harry or Aunt Emma, or discuss the origin of their aches and pains. Although necromancy (to use the classic term for intercourse with spirits) accompanies the history of all higher religions, it has always been understood as a crooked path fraught with dangers for its practitioners. Spiritual apparitions such as Paul experienced on the road to Damascus are born of God's love for man, while necromancy is born of less lofty motives. God spoke to man through Old Testament prophets and through Christ for the sake of humanity. Those who desire to consort with so-called entities are not motivated by such all-encompassing love. But more important, their chief concern is not with God's will as it is revealed in Christ.

There are a few today who would deny that the cosmos is throbbing with life. And who would limit life to that which is seen? Neither Judaism nor Christianity deny the existence of spirits. King Saul consulted the witch of Endor who evoked the spirit of Samuel for him, although necromancy and witchcraft were forbidden (Lev. 19:31; Deut 18:11). Christ exorcised evil spirits on many occasions, but in the case of the epileptic son (Mk. 9:14-27) not even his disciples could drive out the spirit but only he himself (Mk. 9:28-29). There may be demons and angels, good and bad spirits, but they exist in a realm extraneous to ours, with which man should not tamper. Paul spoke of vast realms, thrones, dominions, principalities and authorities (Col. 1:16), but he warned of a danger few present-day spiritualists are willing to recognize, that "even Satan disguises himself as an angel of light" (II Cor. 11:14). Christianity traditionally discouraged intercourse with spirits, not because it doubted their existence, but because such was understood to be contrary to the counsel of God, the eternal Spirit.

ESP conducts experiments with cards or dice and employs statistical methods of evaluation. Spiritualists, on the other hand, employ entirely subjective methods to achieve contact with entities, such as table-tipping, automatic writing and the planchette, or ouija board. The most ancient method known is that of a medium, a person gifted with psychic powers, who goes into a trance, or catatonic sleep. In this state his conscious mind and free will are suspended. His body is then used by the entity who speaks through his voice box. The entity assumes a proper name for identification purposes and answers questions directed to it by people other than the medium who is asleep. Neither the medium nor the participants at a séance can possibly be sure of the origin, quality and intent of the entity.

Mr. David H. Cole, a young Universalist minister of wide intellectual interests, recently attended a séance in Chicago conducted by Mr. Ford, the famous trance medium, for a gathering of ten ministers. Through the voice of Mr. Ford an entity calling himself "Fletcher" addressed the gathering on topics uppermost in their minds. The remarks of this entity, however, were so general and platitudinous that nothing could be derived of either a practical or inspirational value. This is symptomatic of most séances, particularly those approached from a devotional angle. Those who wait with bated breath for new revelations in spiritistic séances do not have a "ghost of a chance."

That mediums have stunned many people with knowledge of intimate details of their lives is well known. There is a faculty at work of which we know nothing as yet. The spiritistic hypothesis, while not entirely ruled out, has, however, one great inherent weakness. In his autobiography *Nothing So Strange,* written in collaboration with Margueritte Harmon Bro, Mr. Ford wrote that entities appearing at a séance are "loved ones of the sitter," thus explaining the intensely personal and subjective nature of the material received. But many communications from so-called spirit guides contradict experience (such as their claim of reincarnating) and they pervert the teachings of Christianity with a sentimental relativism indicating a background in eastern occultism and metaphysics on the part of the mediums. But Paul warned: ". . . even if we, or an angel from heaven, should preach to you a gospel contrary to that which we preached to you, let him be accursed" (Gal. 1:8).

Prayer is resorted to rarely by professional mediums. In prayer the mind and the emotions, in short, the whole consciousness of the individual, is at a higher pitch, which automatically cancels out the possibility of an entity taking control of the body. On the contrary, during the Middle Ages and before, prayer was used as an effective protection against spirits and demons. Psychic research has shown that an entity cannot manifest without some cooperation by the medium and the means he provides, such as nervous energy (mediums are usually utterly exhausted after a séance), his voice to speak with, or his hands to write with. As every seasoned psychic investigator knows, it is more often that the entity seems to need help rather than the person who appeals to it. The Roman Catholic doctrine of Intercession is based upon the belief in the survival of the soul. But even the saints cannot help directly those who pray to them, but intercede for them with Christ.

Those who desire "proof" of the survival of the soul too readily accept the claims of any entity (or medium) to be their deceased relative. The messages received during séances are so subjective that it is wiser to maintain an attitude of extreme caution toward all claims of having communed with a specific entity. The powers of the subconscious are as yet too little known and it is therefore quite possible that in most alleged communications from a recently deceased person the desire to speak with him again prompted the phenomena. Schrenck-Notzing came to this conclusion after a lifetime of studying parapsychology: "A medium may honestly believe that a spirit is manifesting itself through her or through him when, as a matter of fact, the manifestation is directed solely through a subdivision of her own ego in the subconscious."

Spiritualism is the no-man's land between ESP and authentic religious-visionary experiences. Its adherents have marshalled the theories of yoga, Zen, magic, theosophy, and Dr. Carl J. Jung for philosophical support, producing a pseudo-science and religious syncretism similar to Gnosticism. Instead of penetrating the mysteries of Christianity, spiritualists seem to be moving further away. One of the greatest gifts Christianity gave to mankind was freedom from dependence upon and fear of psychic forces. In the words of Paul, "Formerly, when you did not know God, you were in bondage to beings that by nature are no gods; but now that you have come to know God, or rather to be known by

God, how can you turn back again to the weak and beggarly elemental spirits, whose slaves you want to be once more?" (Gal. 4:8-9).

The attempt to utilize the powers of entities or to communicate with them for selfish and petty ends is not only a denial of the potential of faith, but turns back the clock to a prehistoric level of religion when shamans and wizards ruled the life of their tribes with "familiars." Christ chased demons and spirits out the front door — are they going to be let in again through the back? It remains to be seen what spiritualism will accomplish that deep faith cannot. Spiritualists are mystics without faith. Those who need phenomena to support their faith do well to recall Christ's words to Thomas: "Blessed are those who have not seen and yet believe."

Zen-Buddhism

LIT-SEN CHANG

ZEN Buddhism is not without some plausible features, which explains why some people become its easy prey.

1. Take, for example, *its protest against rationalism and humanism:* "Mere scholasticism or mere sacerdotalism . . . will never create a living faith. The intellect is useful in its place, but when it tries to cover the whole field of religion, it dries up the source of life" (William Barrett, ed., *Zen Buddhism, Selected Writings of D. T. Suzuki,* pp. 111, 112, 114,). "Man has followed rationalism to the point where rationalism has transformed itself into its utter irrationality" (E. Fromm, et. al., *Zen Buddhism and Psychoanalysis,* pp. 78, 79; also Fromm, *Psychoanalysis and Religion,* pp. 6, 7). Or, "The present time is the age of humanism, in which the human being is the scale of all things. Here his task is to liberate himself from various fetters or bondages. It is a modern characteristic, especially in the West, that man is the master of life" (Sohaku Ogata, *Zen for the West,* pp. 16, 17).

Lit-sen Chang is Lecturer in Oriental Religions in Gordon Divinity School. A native Chinese, he studied law in University of Paris and is author of numerous texts on legal themes. Formerly he was Professor in National Central University, Nanking, National Chi-nan University, Shanghai, and Soochow University Law School, Shanghai, and President of Kaingnan University. A convert from Buddhism, he holds the B.D. from Gordon.

2. *It teaches egolessness and "great death."* According to the doctrines of Wu-chu (non-abiding) and Wu-nieng (no thoughts), "our individual consciousness, merged into the unconscious, must become like the body of a dead man." "Let your mind be like vacuity of space, like a chip of dead wood and a piece of stone, like cold ashes and burnt-out coal." "All the doings and happenings, including thoughts and feelings, which I have or which come to me, are of the divine will as long as there are on my part no clingings, no hankerings, and my mind is wholly disconnected with things of the past, present and future" (Barret, *op cit.*, pp. 197, 198, 200). The great death is the ego dying to itself in its radical negativity. In no sense, however, is this depicted as a nihilistic destruction or expiration into a hollow void or nothingness. "In dying to itself as ego, it is born and awakens to itself as self" (Fromm, et al., *op. cit.*, p. 167).

3. *It casts dim light on man's way and life.* Some Zen scholars often employ biblical verses or terms to illustrate or express their aspiration about way and life. "It is at once the Life, the Truth and the Way" (C. Humphreys, *Zen Buddhism*, p. 1). "The Truth shall make you free" (Fromm, *Psychoanalysis and Religion*, pp. 6, 7). "As if walking in the Garden of Eden" (D. T. Suzuki, *An Introduction to Zen Buddhism*, p. 45). "He that loseth his life shall find it" (A. W. Watts, *The Spirit of Zen*, p. 60). "Let thy will be done." "Take no thought for the morrow" (Barret, *op. cit.*, p. 200). "Before Abraham was, I am" (*ibid.*, p. 239). "Except a man be born again, he cannot see the Kingdom of God." "Neither circumcision availeth anything nor uncircumcision, but a new creature." "Forget those things which are behind." "The Spirit of God dwelleth in us." "For us the body is one" (cf. Robert Linssen (*Living Zen*, pp. 204-223).

While, however, Zen gains plausibility from some of its teachings, it is nevertheless objectionable because of its serious inadequacy and sheer futility.

SERIOUS INADEQUACY OF ZEN

1. *It supersedes the doctrine of a real Creator.* Zen is a peculiar and subtle form of atheism. By identifying deity with nature, it denies the infinity and transcendence of a living personal God. All visible objects thus become but modifications of self-existence, of an unconscious and impersonal essence which is called God, Nature, the Absolute, Oneness, Suchness, or Tathagata, and so on. This robs God of sovereignty by denuding him of his power of self-determination in relation to the world. God is reduced to the hidden ground. Since Zen does not affirm the existence of the living God, it is not only absolutely destitute of the special revelation of God in his Word but is wholly alien to the God of revelation. Since Zen contends that it does not deny the existence of God, it is more plausible in its pretension, more fascinating to the imagination, and less revolting to the reason than those colder and coarser theories which ascribe the origin of the world to mere mechanical laws of matter and motion. Besides, Zen adopts the very language of theism, and may even generate a certain mystic piety; statements are often embellished with the charms of seductive eloquence, and become the formidable rival of Christian theism.

2. *It engenders a spirit of mysticism.* Zen has a strong tendency to breed mysticism through its resort to the doctrines of radical intuition, that is, its requirement of "no dependence upon words and letters"; of "special transmission of the Mind"; of "seeing into one's own nature"; of revolt against reason. Ogata, in

his *Zen for the West,* says, "I see much common ground in Zen and the mysticism of Meister Eckhart, as he wrote, 'The eye by which I see God is the same eye by which God sees me. My eye and God's eye are one and the same — one in seeing, one in knowing and one in loving.' . . . When I have shut the doors of my five senses, earnestly desiring God, I find him in my soul as clearly and as joyful as he is in eternity. . . . Meditation, high thinking and union with God, have drawn me to heaven" (pp. 17-19).

Charles Hodge reminds us that "there is a sense in which the Spirit is given to every man. He is present with every human mind exciting to good, restraining from evil. Without this common grace, or general influence of the Spirit, there would be no difference between our world and hell." But, he stresses, "the fact that the Spirit is present with every human mind, and constantly enforces the truth to that mind, is no proof that He makes immediate supernatural revelations to every human being. The fact is, we cannot see without light. It is vain to say that every man has an inward light sufficient to guide him without the sun. Facts are against the theory. . . . To tell men, therefore, to look within for an authoritative guide and to trust to their irresistible convictions, is to give them a guide which will lead them to destruction!" (*Systematic Theology,* I, pp. 101, 102).

3. *It disregards the holiness of God.* In Zen's conception, sin against God does not exist. It boldly declares that the "immaculate Yogins do not enter Nirvana and the precept-violating monks do not go to hell. To avoid sin and evil by obedience to any moral law is only an idle attempt. Every being must act according to the Nature." "There is . . . no need of rules of morality" (Humphreys, *op. cit.,* pp. 178, 179). Imma-

ture disciples make this all-inclusiveness of Zen an excuse for pure libertinism (Watts, *op. cit.*, p. 61). Dr. Karl L. Reichelt, an experienced missionary sympathetic to Buddhism, observes that "as a general rule, those who have 'broken through' rise well above average, although they do not measure up to the truly Christian standard; but greed for power and honour is on the whole unshaken." On the other hand, some of these people develop very odd qualities. The Chinese humorously say that they have become "mo-wong" (demon king), which means they are mentally deranged (Reichelt, *Meditation and Piety in the Far East*, pp. 14, 15). Many ludicrous anecdotes are found in the autobiographies of Zen masters (cf. Chang Chen-chi, *The Practice of Zen*, pp. 34, 40, 85-114). In the West, some of the "Beatniks" (although altogether immature in their understanding of Zen) reflect its influence (cf. John Kerouac, *The Dharma Bums*).

4. *It denies the need of a Saviour.* Zen is a radical form of auto-soterism or self-salvation. In it "there is no supernatural intervention, way or refuge. We bear the whole responsibility for our actions and no Sage whosoever he be has the right to encroach on our free will. . . . Only ignorance, laziness and cowardice can lead us to seek outside aid. One thing seems fundamentally necessary: 'To know ourselves.' If we attain the perfectly clear vision of what we are, we no longer need 'to go elsewhere.' The exterior ways become to us ways of perdition. Just as all men and women of all the people of the earth have said and will say at the moment of their Awakening, so do we say simply, 'I am the way.'" (Linssen, *op. cit.*, pp. 73-75). This teaching must surely result in self-deification, which is the basic characteristic and serious fallacy of heathenism.

UTTER FAILURE OF ZEN

1. In "seeing into one's own nature" Zen fails to recognize that self-knowledge is rather twofold: first, the condition in which man was at first created: and second, his condition since Adam's fall. Ever since Adam revolted from the fountain of righteousness, all the parts of the soul have been possessed by sin. The nature of man, in both intellect and will, requires regeneration of the Spirit. Romans 3:10-18 depicts our human nature as vicious not simply by custom (or as some modern Zen scholars put it in terms of so-called "force of habit", Linssen, *op. cit.*, pp. 103-106), but rather perpetually corrupted. Therefore,instead of "seeing into one's own nature," our need is for a new nature and for the Spirit of God to form in us anew the image of God which was marred by the transgression of Adam.

2. In the attainment of Enlightenment, Zen ignores the Pauline declaration in I Corinthians 2:5 that "your faith should not stand in the wisdom of man, but in the power of God." Calvin reminds us that "had Adam stood upright, the course of nature would have conducted us to know God. But in the present ruin of the human race, no one will now perceive God to be either a Father, or the Author of salvation, until Christ interpose to make our peace" (*Institutes,* I, ii, 2).

Although Zen asserts that without "Satori" (Enlightenment), "Zen is a sealed book" (Barrett, *op. cit.*, p. 135), the actual fact is that apart from divine revelation, "Satori" can never be genuine. Even a psychologist as sympathetic to Zen as Dr. Carl G. Jung says, "We can never decide definitely whether a person is really enlightened, or whether he merely imagines it; we have no criterion of this." These words of Jung actually appear in the foreword of *An Introduction to*

Zen Buddhism, by Suzuki, greatest living authority of Zen Buddhism.

Although Zen professes to open a "third eye" (Barrett, *op. cit.,* p. 3), we recall Augustine's statement that "the mental eye remains shut until it is opened by the Lord" (*De Peccat. Merit. et Remiss.,* II, v). Because "the god of this world hath blinded the minds of them which believe not" (II Cor. 4:4), Zen in fact is truly "a sealed book."

3. In respect to the way of salvation, Zen does not offer what the Christian religion of redemption offers. This is clear, first, from the basic nature of "Satori" (Enlightenment). Satori always requires a certain amount of subconscious incubation. It is said that a merely chance occurrence — a sight, a sound — may bring it about. Often it is accompanied by intense emotional phenomena such as a trembling, a rush of tears, or a cold sweat. A typical example was the experience of Pai-chang Huai-hai (724-814), "after his master Matsu abruptly took hold of his nose, and gave it a twist. This made his back wet with cold perspiration. He was said to have 'Satori'" (Barrett, *op. cit.,* p. 92). Another example was that of Yun-men (Ummon). When he was pushed out of the gate of his master, one of his legs was caught and broken. It is said the intense pain resulting from this awakened him, and he had "Satori" (*ibid.,* p. 12). This indicates, Jung asserts, that Satori is a "psychological problem." But a psychology which ignores true spiritual values is doomed to fail. As Christ profoundly said, some new affection of expulsive power from on high must be instilled when the house of life is swept and garnished, lest the former occupant return with seven others worse than himself (J. A. C. Murray, *An Introduction to a Christian Psychotherapy,* p. 12). Our only hope is the

One Great Physician, the One Great Psychiatrist, whose work and power can heal the disorders of our restless psyche.

Secondly, according to Linchi (Renzai), Zen is no other than the Mind. Zen is known as "Hsin-tsung," the discipline of mind. Thus "Zen demands will power," Jung asserts in his foreword to Suzuki's book. But Zen is ignorant of the serious fact that without the power of the Holy Spirit the will of man is not free. Having been made a captive, the will can do nothing in the way of righteousness.

Thirdly, Satori is not regeneration, not conversion. Dr. Reichelt asserts, "the attainment of cosmic consciousness (Satori) does not touch the deepest levels of human life. It does not generally reach down to the depths of conscience in its relation to God. Although a 'cosmic awakening' may bring a certain clarity and peace of mind to a man . . . the life of faith has not been kindled at all, because the object of faith is vague and unhistorical, it is all veiled in the mist of pantheism" (*op. cit.*, pp. 16, 17). Moreover, since Zen is a revolt against any authority and it does not affirm the existence of God nor the need of a Saviour, it has no object of faith. Its purposes to discipline the mind and make it its own master, through seeing into one's own nature. Although Zen masters claim "certain similarities between Satori and the sudden conversion of Christianity" (Watts, *op, cit.*, p. 76), there is in fact no ground for comparison. In their own words they say, "conversion is held to come to essentially depraved man from an external God, while Satori is the realization of one's own inmost nature. . . . It is one's own spiritual realization that makes the difference and the mind is its own place, and of itself can make a heaven of hell, a hell of heaven" (*ibid.*, pp. 79, 80).

Fourthly, while Zen is defined as the "unity of man and the universe," as the "rhythm of the mind with the changing forms," and as "a state of One-ness" (*ibid.*, p. 121), Zen masters strongly advocate such doctrines as nonduality, nondiscrimination, and non-differentiation. Zen thus distorts the biblical truth by ignoring the gravest factor in the history of mankind, namely, the fall of Adam, by which the ground is cursed and our sorrows are multiplied (cf. Gen. 3:16-19). It is true, Adam's spiritual life was originally united and bound to his Maker; but his estrangement and his revolt against God perverted the whole order of nature in heaven and earth and deteriorated his race. Zen masters, like other philosophers, only tell us to live in harmony with nature; but the Bible enjoins us to regulate our lives with a view to God to whom nature belongs.

Fifthly, salvation is the plan of God before the foundation of the world, not a man-made system of philosophy or religion. It is the wisdom of God, not a wisdom of man. "For no man hath ascended up to heaven, but he that came down from heaven, even the Son of man, which is in heaven" (John 3:13). God, in his infinite mercy, having determined to redeem us, became himself our Redeemer in the power of his only begotten Son.

SELECTION OF BOOKS FOR STUDY

William Barrett, editor, *Zen Buddhism — Selected Writings of D. T. Suzuki* (Doubleday, 1956).

John Blofeld (tr.), *The Zen Teaching of Huang Po*, (Grove Press, 1959).

R. H. Blyth, *Zen in English Literature and Oriental Classics* (Charles Tuttle, 1957).

Chen-chi Chang, *The Practice of Zen* (Harper, 1959).

E. Fromm, D. T. Suzuki and R. DeMartino, *Zen Buddhism and Psycholanalysis* (Harper, 1960).

Chiokao Fujisawa, *Zen and Shinto* (Philosophical Library, 1959).

C. Humphreys, *Zen Buddhism* Allen and Unwin, (London, 1957).

Wu-chi Lien, *A Short History of Confucian Philosophy* (Penguin Books, 1955).

Robert Linssen, *Living Zen,* (Tr. by D. Abrahams-Curiel) (Grove Press, 1958).

Sohaku Ogata, *Zen for the West* (Dial Press, 1959).

Karl L. Reichelt, *Meditation and Piety in the Far East* (Harper, 1954).

D. T. Suzuki, *Essays in Zen Buddhism,* 3 vols. Rider. (London, 1949, 1950, 1951).

D. T. Suzuki, *An Introduction to Zen Buddhism* (Philosophical Library, 1949).

D. T. Suzuki, *Manual of Zen Buddhism* (Grove Press, 1960).

A. W. Watts, *The Spirit of Zen* (Grove Press, 1958).

A. W. Watts, *The Way of Zen* (Pantheon, 1957).

A. W. Watts, *The Way of Liberation in Zen Buddhism* American Academy of Asian Studies (San Francisco, 1955).

The Challenge of the Cults*

Since the advent of Christian missionary activities on an organized scale some two hundred years ago, the proclamation of the Gospel message has faced many problems. Obstacles of language, culture, race, militant nationalism and the competition between missionaries of differing doctrinal persuasion have contributed a stormy atmosphere to world missions.

In addition to these difficulties, major non-Christian religions (such as Islam, Buddhism, Hinduism, Taoism, Shintoism) have actively opposed Christian missionaries so that progress has been slow not in a few areas and in some instances hardly recognizable.

Beyond this aspect, however, looms another formidable adversary, the rise of non-Christian American cults. Some of these movements have lately invaded established missionary fields and have proselytized new converts with startling success. Utilizing some methods reminiscent of early Christianity, these groups cater to the culture patterns of those they proselytize, provide literature in the language of the people and in one way or another keep a certain emphasis on the Bible in the forefront of their work. In many instances they preach a militant "separatism" from tobacco, alcohol, and other practices classified as worldly and unspiritual. All these activities are bolstered by their so-called revelations (all of nineteenth century vintage), with an appeal to which they wage unceasing warfare against all religions and against Christian denominations in particular. It is significant that they first approach known Christians. Seldom do they attempt to

* Editorial from the December, 19, 1960 issue of *Christianity Today*.

reach the unevangelized, which should be the first step in any genuine missionary program.

•

We are not suggesting that the activities of these movements be curtailed by law, or that they should become the target of an evangelical barrage of abuse. Full freedom of worship and the right to promulgate one's convictions are historic planks in the platform of Protestant evangelism. Even such terms as "sect" or "cult" seem more appropriate in lands with a state church than in an open religious situation. But Christianity will need to preserve the distinction between truth and heresy if it is to have a future.

Some groups, particularly Jehovah's Witnesses, by their demonstrated hostility to governmental authorities, have frequently jeopardized the reputation and efforts of others of genuine Christian persuasion. As a result there has been great friction between their workers and Christian missionaries. It is difficult indeed for Christian missionaries successfully to compete with such divisive forces in a positive way, and to evangelize missionaries of such zealous groups as the Mormons, Jehovah's Witnesses and virulent indigenous groups.

•

Foremost in the missionary programs of the cults is an emphasis upon the Bible. Despite the prominence given the Scriptures, however, the cults, without exception, place themselves in the role of infallible interpreters of the Word of God with a vengeance rivaled only in dogmatism by Roman Catholicism. The Mormons, for instance, insist that the Scriptures be interpreted in the light of the *Book of Mormon, The Pearl of Great Price,* and *Doctrine and Covenants,* the supposedly inspired oracles of the Church of Jesus Christ of Latter-Day Saints. Jehovah's Witnesses elevate the *Watchtower* and *Awake* magazines and other publications of the Watch Tower Society to the position of supreme interpreter. Christian Scientists subject the Scriptures to the vagaries of Mary Baker Eddy's writings. Instead of being "the infallible rule of faith and practice," the Bible is relegated to a secondary position. This is accomplished almost subliminally, so that the convert is unaware that his primary authority is not really grounded in Scripture but rather in the interpretation of Scripture by the respective cults.

The Living Word of God, the Lord Jesus Christ, is treated similarly in the theologies of the major cults. For Jehovah's Witnesses he becomes a super angel (Michael) and during his earthly ministry a "perfect man." In the theology of the Mormons our Lord becomes in his pre-existence a "brother" of Satan and one of many gods which occupy the worlds scattered throughout the celestial galaxies. Among the gnostic cults (Christian Science, Unity, Christ Unity Science, Religious Science, New Thought, and so on) the Son of God becomes the "Christ idea" an emanation or projection from the Divine Mind, a partaker of the essence of God (the I Am) of which all men are the possessors because they are "God's children" and "the reflections of the divine idea." The cults know no triune God, no incarnate Word, no vicarious sacrifice and no risen Saviour in the sense of historical biblical theology. And, sad to say, their views are being promulgated on every major mission field with a steady flow of literature.

Consider the fact that Jehovah's Witnesses alone has ventured a major offensive against almost all other missions, and that their magazine, *The Watchtower*, has grown from 6,000 in 1879 to over 3 million copies per month in 46 languages in 1960. *The Watchtower's* second largest publication, *Awake,* has reached 22 million copies per year in 18 languages. Their growing mission force of full and part-time workers is reliably estimated in excess of 200,000 persons actively propagating the theocratic kingdom of "Pastor" Russell and the late Judge Rutherford. During the years 1942 to 1952 membership in Jehovah's Witnesses doubled in North America, multiplied fifteen times in South America, twelve times in the Atlantic islands, five times in Asia, seven times in Europe and Africa, and six times in the islands of the Pacific. Now, the close of an eight-year period, the Watch Tower's membership has far exceeded these figures, and indications reveal stronger missionary threats yet to come.

In South America, particularly Brazil, we have seen a resurgence of Spiritism on an unprecedented scale. *Time* magazine devoted its religious section not long ago to comments by a Roman Catholic missionary deploring the inroads of the Spiritists on the Roman Catholic church. Unfortunately the same can be said also in respect to some Protestant agencies.

Added to the major American-based cultic systems are certain indigenous cults with strong nationalistic overtones, particularly in Africa and Asia. These groups amalgate some of the teachings of Christianity with the older pagan religions, particularly Animism and Spiritism, and come equipped complete with their own special revelations and messiahs. This situation is particularly true in the Philippine Islands, Japan, and Africa where Christianity is caricatured as the "white man's religion," a Western "import" superimposed on native cultural and religious patterns. Such an approach has been disastrously successful.

Another major cult gaining tremendous prestige and

publicity throughout the world is Moral Rearmament, better known and advertised as MRA. Headed by the now aging Dr. Frank Buchman, and emphasizing a five-fold platform for the moral rehabilitation of mankind as opposed to the atheistic ideology of communism, MRA cuts across denominational and even major religious boundaries to enlist support against the atheistic materialism of communism. MRA in many quarters has become a rallying point for those who wish to oppose communism and still maintain religious affiliations and fellowship with like-minded sympathizers regardless of race or creed. It is conveniently forgotten that MRA is the evolution of the old Oxford group movement which started out as an essentially Christian movement of extreme mystical character. It eventually degenerated into an homogenization of all religions in which the exclusive claims of Jesus Christ, whose gospel Dr. Buchman in his Lutheran ordination vows (never renounced) swore to preach and defend, are conveniently lost in the shuffle or else totally rejected. Those who eagerly embrace MRA chiefly for its religio-political opposition to communism might do well to look into the political history of this movement, which has numbered among its most faithful supporters some of the most militant fascists in England, Europe, and America.

Another force on growing mission fields is that of the Seventh-day Adventist denomination which, while giving large emphasis to Christian truth, tends to proselytize on a large scale, using the so-called "special truths" of the Advent message as a lever to pry Christians of other denominations away from their place of fellowship. Reports from world mission fields indicate that although the Adventists are attempting to meet this problem on a high level, so-called "grass root" adherents are guilty of divisive practices and still wield considerable authority in certain areas. Answers must therefore be provided to Sabbatarianism, soul sleep and the annihilation of the wicked, the prophetic office of Ellen G. White, the investigative judgment and the sanctuary doctrines, dogmas which are actively promulgated by Seventh-day Adventism.

On the basis of past performance, it is safe to prognosticate that within the next decade, all things remaining constant, the cults will intensify their propaganda and their "sheep stealing" activities three to four times their present rate. The question is, will the Church of Jesus Christ rise to the occasion while there remains time? The Church must be prepared to defend the claim of Scripture, interpreted by the Holy Spirit, that it *alone* is "inspired by God and profitable for doctrine, for reproof, for correction and for instruction in righteousness" (II Tim. 3:16), and that the Holy Spirit thereby bringing to our remembrance "all things" that Christ has commanded us, is a far safer guide than the extra-biblical revelations of cult leaders.

The Christian Church must also be ever ready to remind indigenous nationalistic sects that Christianity is an Eastern religion, that Christ was born, died, rose, and ascended in Asia, and that his return will be to the Mount of Olives in Asia from which he ascended to the right hand of the Father as our advocate.

•

Finally, if the cults are to be effectively combatted at home and on the foreign mission fields of the world, missionaries, pastors, educators, and interested laymen must press for strong curricula in our educational institutions. Christians must be taught not only *what* they believe but *why* they believe, that they may be able, as Scripture admonishes us, "to give to everyone that asks of you a reason for the hope that is in you" (I Pet. 3:15).

The teachings of the major sects must be codified and indexed, and a running commentary provided for all interested parties. It will then be possible to understand the methodology of the cults at home and abroad, to note the areas of their doctrinal emphasis and their use and abuse of the Word of God. The Church of Jesus Christ has nothing to fear from the zeal and competition of the cults. She has much to fear from her own apathy and lethargy in this vital area of missionary concern. The means to evangelize and to combat adherents of the cult is available. On every front the Church is faced with unrelenting and mounting pressures from anti-Christian forces. "The night is coming wherein no one can work." The challenge is here, the time is now.